Manifesting From The Inside Out

Create Unlimited Abundance
Through Aligning Your Heart, Mind,
and Spirit

Anna Anderson

"You are not a drop
in the ocean. You are
the entire ocean in a
drop."

- Rumi

CONTENTS

INTRODUCTION

Are you manifesting the life you want - or the life you are unconsciously settling for?

Everything you've ever desired, dreamed of, or yearned for already exists for you. It's not just possible; it's meant for you. The Universe wants it for you because your light, your truth, and your gifts matter deeply. This book is here to remind you of your magnificence. And when I say magnificence, I mean **<u>MAGNIFICENCE</u>** in all caps, bold, and underlined.

You are here for a reason - a unique and profound reason. You hold a frequency that only you can bring to the world. And as you come home to that truth, your frequency will influence a change in the world.

Yes, you are that powerful: your thoughts and your experiences influence the entire Universe because everything about you is vibrational. You are far from an island… you are part of the collective. And as you come home to your divinity and remember who you really are, you will remember that not only can you transform your world and live your dreams, you also have the ability to bring peace to this planet. Simply living in alignment with your truth will shift our collective vibration. I like to think of us all as little lamps, scattered across the world, connected through an unseen web of light. And as each one of us remembers, as each one of us awakens to the truth of who we are, the lamp ignites. One by one, we light up. One by one, we come home to ourselves.

So yes, your dreams matter. More than you know.

Because when you step into the life you are here to live, when you listen to the pull of your soul and follow where it leads, you don't just change your world. You light your lamp. And that in turn contributes to the network of us all. Together, coming home to our hearts will transform the world.

Your deepest desires are not random. They are your soul calling you home. Your dreams matter because they are what you came here to realise.

Let these words settle in your heart: *You are important. You are significant. You are deeply loved and you are POWERFUL.* No amount of success in the physical world will ever make you matter more or less - you already matter, infinitely. If you truly knew this, you'd never settle for less than what you deserve.

However, chances are, you've been conditioned to measure your worth through your achievements. You've placed emphasis on external markers of success, forgetting that your true power lies within. While what you achieve in the physical world doesn't define you, wouldn't it be wonderful to live with ease, joy, and abundance? To master this physical experience and create a life that feels aligned, free, and deeply fulfilling? This is your birthright.

If this message is all you take from this book - great! You're already on the path. But if you're curious about how to embody this truth and create the life you dream of, stick with me. That's what this journey is about - coming home to yourself, breaking old patterns, and living a life that reflects the beauty of who you are. Know this:

- Where there is a will, there is a way.
- Where there is a desire, there is a path.
- Where there is a dream, there is also the power to create it.

Why else would you have the dream? In fact, the dream is the beginning of the process of creation - it all starts with an idea. Just think, anything that has ever been created began in someone's imagination. Therefore, all of your ideas are entirely possible for you. You are never given anything that you can't achieve. It may take effort, it may require you to step out of your comfort zone, but if you dare to be bold and believe in yourself, it is entirely possible for you to create the life of your dreams.

Your discomfort with not having what you desire right now is actually a GOOD thing. If you were content with everything in your life, you would not have purchased this book and that means you would be settling.

But that is not you, is it? You KNOW there is more, you KNOW there is another level for you. And you are correct. So lean into your discomfort, and get OK with having desires. These are GOOD things - they are the fuel that makes you hungry for change and the signposts directing you where to go.

> *"The privilege of a lifetime is being
> who you truly are."*
> - Joseph Campbell

Here's something important to know: my job is simply to remind you. The words you'll read in this book are not new to you - they are a gentle awakening to the truths already encoded in your DNA. Your Soul has always known what I'm about to share. In fact, it was your Soul that nudged you to pick up this book, to say "yes" to reconnect with the wisdom that has always been yours.

What I am about to share with you is something you already know deep within your core. This book is your guide to remembering. My intention is for these words to feel like coming home. Coming home to the truth, coming home to *your* truth.

You may have forgotten this, but the truth is, you are Spirit. You are an eternal being having a physical experience. On your path through eternity, there are certain projects for you to master along the way - things you need to learn and understand before you are able to forge forward to the next level. That is why you are here. You are here to master this physical world. You are here to learn how to manipulate energy and to create your reality around you.

Before you came here, you were excited about this opportunity. You chose certain experiences and lessons - your contracts - to help you grow and evolve. These are not random; they are purposeful. These contracts reside in what is called the Akashic records. The Akashic is a mental plane of yet to be manifested potential that has your name written on it!

In a nutshell, you are a divine and eternal being and you came here for a reason - a reason that your Soul knows and is logged and stored on another plane. You are here for a period of time to learn how to master this physical density and to fulfil those contracts you chose. You also have guides and angels - your team of light - supporting you every step of the way. You have a direct channel to your higher self to guide you along your journey.

As part of this human experience, you were also granted something incredibly powerful: free will. The right to choose. Do you fulfil your contracts, or do you choose something else? Do you listen to your inner wisdom, or do you allow the chatter of your mind to lead the way? This is the essence of being human - the ability to choose the life you wish to lead.

From my perspective, the world has forgotten its divinity. We have moved so far away from our spiritual nature that much of humanity operates from a place of fear and separation. From birth, we are programmed to compete, to survive, to believe in lack. We are told that hard work and suffering are the only paths to success, that our worth lies in what we achieve rather than who we are.

Life doesn't need to be like this. It really doesn't.

"You are the Universe, expressing itself as a human for a little while."
- Eckhart Tolle

That's what this book is about - how to manifest the life you were born to live. The life where you are in alignment with your truth, living in flow, abundance, health, wealth, joy, and love. You don't need to chase after things to feel good enough. You truly don't. These words are an invitation to come home to your inner wisdom and trust that the infinite Universe is ready to support you. You are capable of creating the life of your dreams - it is entirely possible for you.

Are you ready? Let's dive in.

MY STORY

*"At any moment, you have a choice,
that either leads you closer to your
spirit or further away from it."*
- Thich Nhat Hanh

Before we go any further, I will share a little about me. You might be wondering how I came to know this truth and how I shifted from living in limitation to creating a life of alignment. Let me take you back to the beginning.

If you've read my first book, *From The Inside Out*, you already know a lot about me, so I'll keep this short. But I want to give you some context about why I'm writing this book and why I've dedicated my life to sharing this message with as many people as possible.

I grew up in Devon and had a relatively normal childhood. My parents separated when I was eight years old, it was messy, complicated but there was never a question I was deeply loved and cared for. My parents worked hard to provide for us and whilst there were challenges, we were fortunate in many ways. However, somewhere along the line, I picked up a belief (as I know that many of us do) that the only measure of my worth was what I had created or achieved outside of myself. A belief embedded deep within me that I, in my own right, was not good enough.

That belief shaped how I viewed myself and the world. In *From The Inside Out*, I share how this belief manifested in my relationship with my body. I thought, *If I can look a certain way, then I'll be good enough.* So I binged, purged, starved, compared, judged, and obsessed over every aspect of my appearance. My external image became my measure of self-worth.

But this belief didn't stop at my body. It seeped into every corner of my life - my relationships, career, finances, and decisions. I sought validation constantly, terrified of being exposed as "not enough." I worked hard to tick every box I thought I was supposed to tick: excelling at school, going to university, landing a job in the city of London. Yet beneath it all, I was sabotaging myself. I made reckless financial decisions, avoided being alone, and chased approval wherever I could find it. I partied hard, drank heavily, and chose relationships that only deepened my wounds. Deep down, I believed that was all I deserved.

By the time I was 33, I was a single mum, and I was struggling. I loved my little boy deeply; he was my gift from the divine. But his dad and I were locked in a painful custody battle. There were regular fights, and when Isaac went to visit his dad, I felt like a hollow shell. I was tired, alone, and completely lost. And it was my deep lack of self-worth that had led me to this extreme low point.

I hated my job, felt disconnected from my life, and drank to numb the pain of it all - completely unaware that the pain was coming from within me. I felt like a powerless victim to my circumstances.

One Sunday, Isaac was with his dad. I woke up with a pounding hangover, having downed a bottle of gin the day before to escape my misery. A voice inside me whispered: *"You can do better than this. If not for you, then for your son. You can do better."*

I had no idea how to "do better." But that voice wouldn't leave me. So, I did what anyone desperate for answers might do: I googled "jobs for mums." At the top of the search results was an opportunity to buy a yoga franchise. Something deep within me stirred - a knowing I couldn't ignore. It didn't make any sense. I was out of shape, not particularly good at yoga, and financially unstable. Leaving my well-paid city job to start a business doing something I didn't fully understand seemed ludicrous.

But I had reached my breaking point, and I needed a change. The thought of paying someone else to take my son to school every day while I trudged through a job I hated was unbearable. Spending time with him was worth the risk. I had to make it work.

By the end of that day, I had bought a yoga business… on a credit card!

Little did I know, I had just made one of the most magical decisions of my life.

When you have a mortgage to pay and a son to feed, there's no room for failure. I threw myself into making the business work. There was no Plan B.

I started practicing yoga every single day, and it gave me a gift I never expected. The more I practiced, the more my life began to change. Yoga created space - space to slow down, to breathe, to be still. It allowed me to move beyond the unkind stories of my lower mind and into a place of peace I had never known before.

I started taking care of myself - eating better, drinking less, and eventually quitting alcohol altogether. I quit smoking. I began to enjoy my own company and needed less distraction. And for the first time in my life, I felt something I didn't recognise: joy.

I fell in love with what I was doing, and that love began to ripple outward. My business started to thrive. I met the man of my dreams, my now-husband. I wrote my first book, which reached 50,000 women around the world. Within a few years, my life became a "pinch me, is this real?" experience.

The reason? I changed within. My entire vibration shifted, and as a result, my external reality transformed to match it. This profound shift in my life ignited a deep fascination within me. I became passionate about learning more and sharing this transformative knowledge with the world. I wanted everyone to know that they have the power to shift their reality by doing the inner work and that the concept of lack is an illusion.

This desire set me on a magical journey of exploration, leading me to knock on many doors in search of deeper metaphysical truths about how we can transform our lives. That quest eventually guided me to the ancient teachings of the mystery schools and the privilege of training in the sacred lineage of King Salomon. This incredible path has opened doors I never imagined possible, and I can't wait to share this magic with you!

That's why I'm writing this book. That's why I do what I do today. My life was once a train wreck, but it has transformed beyond recognition. If that's possible for me, I *know* it's possible for you.

No matter where you are in your life right now, know this: you have the power to create a completely new experience. It is not only possible - it is your divine birthright. Whatever you've been through, know this: there is nothing you can't overcome. But holding onto blame will only keep you stuck in the same patterns. Acceptance and forgiveness are essential if you want to shift your energy, manifest differently, and truly transform your life.

As you move through this book, you'll begin to see that your entire life is a reflection of what you believe about who you are. If you believe you are unloveable, life will mirror that back to you. If you believe you are unworthy, your reality will reflect that belief. But when you remember who you truly are - when you remember your divinity - everything changes.

Perhaps you can relate to this. Maybe you've experienced moments where life seemed to confirm your deepest doubts about yourself. Maybe you've worked hard, done everything "right," only to find that achieving the goal didn't bring the peace you were searching for. If so, know this - you are not alone. And those beliefs? They are not who you are.

Here's what I didn't understand back then: those beliefs weren't the truth. They felt real, but they were just stories I had told myself. And what I didn't realise was that I had the power to rewrite them.

That realisation changed everything.

It set me on a path to rediscovering my worth - one that ultimately led me here, sharing these truths with you now.

"Out of suffering have emerged the strongest souls; the most massive characters are seared with scars."
- Khalil Gibran

CHAPTER 1

A LITTLE BIT OF ETYMOLOGY

*"In the beginning was the Word,
and the Word was with God, and
the Word was God."*
- John 1:1

Let's begin by looking at the first two letters of the word *manifest*. On their own, they are incredibly rich in meaning. MA means to turn nothing into something and something into something else. These two letters appear in words all related to creation: *mamma, matter, master, mage, magick, mastery, imagine, image, magician...* the list goes on.

I share this with you to show how the reality and truth of manifestation is woven into the fabric of our language, hidden in plain sight. Simply to live is to make manifest. You are manifesting all of the time, not just some of the time. So whilst we are here, on this earthly plain, my view is that you might as well make manifest the things you enjoy rather than the things you don't.

Think of a mother, the ultimate master of manifestation. She takes nothing - pure energy - and transforms it into physical life, the most profound act of creation. In German, the word for mother is *mater*, which closely resembles the English word *matter*. *Mater* transforms nothing into *matter*.

This is the essence of manifestation: the act of creation, turning non-physical energy into physical form. Just as a mother births life, you hold the power to birth your dreams, desires, and intentions into reality.

And while we're on the topic, let's look at the word *magick*, spelled with a K at the end. This is not the stage magic you might think of. The "K" symbolises keys - the keys that unlock mastery of the physical world. A magician holds these keys, mastering metaphysics and the art of self - creation. Through this book, I will share some of these keys to help you unlock your innate wisdom and potential in this extraordinary experience of life.

One more word with hidden meaning - *spelling*. Did you know the word *spelling* originates from the practice of writing spells in a grimoire (a book of spells)? Over time, the word *grimoire* evolved into what we now call *grammar*. The ancients understood that words carry vibration, and when spoken with intention, they direct energy. This is what a spell is: a way to channel energy.

> *"We are what we think. All that we are arises with our thoughts. With our thoughts, we make the world."*
> - Buddha

And that's exactly why you're here - to learn how to harness this power, to master this magick, and to remember your innate ability to manifest and create your life intentionally.

So, what does manifestation actually mean, and more importantly, how do we apply it in our lives to create true abundance? When I say abundance, I'm not just talking about wealth - I mean a flow of health, creativity, joy, love, ease, grace, and freedom as well. After all, living in this state is your natural birthright.

As *A Course in Miracles* reminds us: *"Miracles are natural. When they do not occur, something has gone wrong."* Manifestation is the process of taking non-physical potential - the infinite possibilities that already exist - and flowing them into your physical world.

This is not about wishing or hoping; it's about aligning yourself - your thoughts, feelings, actions, and energy - with the reality you wish to create. You become the conduit through which transformation happens, allowing your entire world to shift.

> *"The magician does not create the magic; the magic is already there. He simply opens the door."*
> - Paulo Coelho

CHAPTER 2

FIRST THINGS FIRST: IT'S ALL ENERGY

"The day science begins to study non-physical phenomena, it will make more progress in one decade than in all the previous centuries of its existence."
- Nikola Tesla

Before we dive into how you make these shifts in your inner world, there are a few foundational ideas we need to lay down - concepts that will shape the rest of our journey together.

As you move forward in your process of creation, you will understand the truths, science, and reality behind what it is you are capable of and how the universe is supporting you in making magick happen. Now, I am no scientist, so what I'll share here is simplified - written in layperson's terms with one goal: to make it easy for you to take these ideas and make them real in your life. My passion is weaving together ancient spiritual wisdom and modern scientific teachings, revealing the magical way they speak the same language.

Here's the most important foundation you'll need to fully understand everything we're about to explore: **everything is energy**.

And when I say everything, I mean *everything*. Your thoughts? Energy. Your emotions? Energy. Your body? Energy. You are energy, and the entire world you live in is an energetic dance.

It might not feel that way when you look at a seemingly solid table or feel the ground beneath your feet, but here's the truth: nothing is as still as it seems. Everything is vibrating, pulsing with energy at different frequencies. And here's where things get really interesting...

If you removed all the empty space inside the atoms that make up the entire human race, every single person on Earth - we would collectively collapse down to the size of a sugar cube.

Yes, really.

Atoms - the very building blocks of your body, your home, your entire world - are 99.9999999% empty space. The tiny fraction of "solid" matter they contain is almost nothing in comparison.

Which means this physical world, the one we take so seriously, the one we base all of our fears, doubts, and limitations on - is mostly nothingness.

So if 99.9999999% of what you think is real is actually empty space, then what is reality really made of?

Energy. Frequency. Consciousness.

This is why manifestation isn't about pushing and striving - it's about learning how to work with energy.

This brings us to the first universal truth: **everything is energy, and everything is vibrational.**

From the tiniest particle to the vastness of the cosmos, all matter - whether physical or non-physical - shares this truth. Within atoms, you'll find photons, neutrons, and electrons, each carrying a vibration, spinning and forming the physical world you perceive through your senses.

You see, touch, taste, smell, and hear the physical world. But here's the thing - there's so much more than what your five senses can perceive.

What about the non-physical world?

This is where things get truly exciting. Beyond the physical matter you can see and touch lies an infinite field of energy. Some call it the quantum field; others call it the Divine.

What I love about the time we live in today is how science is proving what ancient wisdom has always known - the truth of God.

Now, when I mention the word "God," this is not in a dogmatic or religious sense. I am not religious, though I have utter respect if you are. I simply like to go back further - to the wisdom that existed before man created religion. There are many interpretations of God, but at its essence, the Divine is the infinite source of creation, the energy that flows through all things.

And here is the part I want you to truly hear: you are made in the image of this Divine energy. As a divine being, you have come here not only to live but to learn how to create and master the physical world. Within you resides the same creative force that holds the Universe together.

This infinite energy, this Divine field, is a realm of pure potential where all possibilities exist. It is here, in this space, that manifestation begins. By recognising this divine energy within and around you, you open yourself to the infinite possibilities of creation. This is the space where your intention meets potential, and where you can consciously create a life aligned with your highest self (which we will get further into later on!).

Understanding this concept is like putting on a pair of glasses that allow you to see life in an entirely new way. When you grasp that your thoughts, feelings, and intentions are not only energetic but also powerful creators, the way you interact with the world changes forever. The way I think of it is like a simulator. You are an energetic being navigating and creating in this simulated physical world through your thoughts, beliefs, and feelings. The challenge is that humans have been conditioned to focus almost entirely on the physical - on what we have, achieve, or own - losing touch with who we truly are and the infinite possibilities available. We focus on what is already created and that we can perceive with our five physical senses, rather than what is possible and sits in the non-physical, waiting to be directed by us - the creators.

When you focus on what already exists, you create a block in the flow of what is coming next. What you see in the physical realm feels limited and your mind starts to feel that is all that is possible. This therefore results in a cycle where more of the same is created, and your world feels as if it is getting smaller and your dreams are getting further away. But it really, really doesn't need to be like that.

"Everything we call real is made of things that cannot be regarded as real."
- Niels Bohr (Quantum Physicist)

Energy is constantly flowing through you, and it expresses itself in alignment with your beliefs about yourself and what you think is possible. In other words, the life you are experiencing right now is a direct reflection of your inner world - your self-worth, your ideas about what you deserve, and your emotional state.

For example, if you believe that owning the home of your dreams (or insert any of your big desires) will finally make you feel worthy, but deep down, you currently feel undeserving or not good enough, that desire cannot come to you. Why? Because your current energetic state is broadcasting, *I don't deserve it and it is not possible for me to make it happen anyway'*. Manifestation doesn't work by chasing or longing for something external to make you feel whole; it works by aligning your inner state with the feelings and energy of already having it. Only then can it be expressed through you.

The key to manifestation is this:

You have to *match* the energy of what you want. It's not about working harder or hoping endlessly; it's about cultivating the feelings of worthiness, abundance, and joy right now. How you feel *in this moment* - not in some imagined future - is the foundation of what you create.

Still with me? Amazing. Let's go a little deeper.

Around 350 years ago, a man named Sir Isaac Newton - arguably one of the greatest scientific minds of all time - made a groundbreaking discovery: gravity. I'm sure you've heard the story of the apple falling on his head (though whether that actually happened is up for debate!).

Newton's genius was in recognising that the physical world operates in predictable ways, governed by laws that can be measured and understood. His three laws of motion and the law of universal gravitation laid the foundation for modern science. For centuries, these laws have shaped how we understand and interact with the physical world.

But here's where it gets interesting.

While Newton's work is nothing short of brilliant, let's keep in mind - he made these discoveries over three centuries ago. Since then, we've learned something extraordinary: the physical world is only part of the story.

What we now know is that non-physical matter, energy in its purest form, doesn't follow the same rules as the physical world. It behaves in ways that Newton could never have imagined: it's fluid, responsive, and infinite in its possibilities. Understanding this is the key to unlocking your creative power.

A couple of hundred years after Newton, another genius, Albert Einstein, came along and shifted the way we see the world. While his work built on Newton's foundations, it also revolutionised physics. Einstein's famous equation $E=mc2$ revealed that energy and mass are interchangeable. This meant that everything - yes, everything - is energy at its core. He also showed that time and space are not fixed; they're relative, depending on the observer. This opened the door to a new way of understanding reality.

Here's where it gets exciting.

Imagine you've always applied Newtonian thinking to your goals. For example, you want to achieve something significant, and you calculate how much time and effort it will take, just as you'd calculate the time needed to travel from point A to B. You might think, *I want to achieve X, but it will take Y amount of time, and therefore, it's not possible.*

This way of thinking is extremely common - and highly limiting.

Enter the observer effect, one of the most fascinating principles of quantum physics. It tells us that we live in a sea of quantum energy, where everything exists as waves of possibility. When you focus your attention on one of these waves - when you *observe* it - it collapses into a physical particle, shaping reality. And when you stop observing it, it returns to its wave state, full of infinite potential.

Think of it this way: the quantum field is like a canvas of endless possibilities. Your thoughts and intentions are the brushstrokes that bring an image to life. What you focus on becomes your reality.

So effectively, you are a being of light. You have come here to master this physical world. Your job is to understand that you are multidimensional and that what you see before you and what you perceive through your five senses is the result of your previous thinking. Your job is to recognise you are here to manipulate non-physical energy through a high vibrational conductor (you) and based on the quality of this vibration, your physical world will manifest around you accordingly. This is where you really start to see that what you think and feel is the foundational principle shaping the entire quality of your physical experience.

*"The very act of observing
disturbs the system."*
- Werner Heisenberg
(Quantum Physicist)

The Programming of the 3D Matrix

From the moment you were born, you were conditioned to think and believe in a certain way. You were taught to attach meaning to the physical world, to measure yourself by external markers of success, to believe that love must be earned, and to seek validation through achievement.

The matrix is the world we, as humans, have constructed - a reality built on Newtonian principles, where everything appears fixed, predictable, and linear. But as we have already explored, this is only one version of reality. You are a multidimensional being living in a multidimensional universe. You did not come here to fit into a predefined mold; you came to express the fullness of who you are.

And here's the truth: there is so much more than what you currently perceive. You are so much more than the limits you have been taught to believe.

The world you have been programmed to live in tells you that life is linear. That success looks a certain way. That you must hit milestones by a certain age, achieve external success to prove your worth, and avoid failure at all costs.

But none of this is real.

When you step beyond this illusion and recognise yourself as an eternal being, walking this path to grow, to learn, and to come home to the truth of your power, you will see that there is no such thing as failure. The mistakes, the setbacks, the detours - they were never proof of your inadequacy. They were simply experiences, nudging you toward expansion.

There is no one in this world who has achieved greatness without first experiencing loss. This is the nature of duality. Before any great rise, there is a fall. This is the pattern woven into every Hero's Journey, every transformation, every creation.

Loss and gain are two sides of the same coin.

If you have lost, it means there is space to receive. If you have fallen, it means there is an opportunity to rise.

Failure does not exist when you are walking a spiritual path because your worth has never been tied to what you achieve. The physical world does not define you because you are an infinite being, and more is always possible for you.

So if you have been measuring yourself by what you haven't yet done, if you have been believing the story that it's too late, that you have failed, that you are behind - pause. Take a breath.

Nothing is lost. Nothing is ever lost.

You are always standing at the threshold of possibility.

And from here, you can create anything.

If you are judging yourself, your life, where you are now, or where you believe you are stuck, that judgement is shaping your vibration. And your vibration is shaping your reality. You cannot create something new from the energy of self-criticism. The universe responds to what you emit - not just what you wish for, but what you truly believe about yourself and your life. So the moment you free yourself from the weight of failure, of comparison, of thinking you are behind, you shift your energy. And when your energy shifts, your reality follows.

It is time to release the self-judgement and realise the brilliance of who you are so that you can make manifest your dreams from where you are. No matter what has been and gone, no matter where you are now. All is possible.

Let's summarise all this in the simplest of terms...

The entire universe is made of energy, including you. Physical energy behaves relative to time and space, which is why achieving things in the physical world often requires a certain amount of time. However, non-physical energy exists beyond these constraints. In the non-physical, all possibilities already exist. When you learn to align your thoughts, emotions, and beliefs with this infinite field of potential, you unlock the ability to create beyond the limitations of time and space.

Here is where another universal law comes into play: **the Law of Duality.** The universe is a vast field of energy that encompasses both the physical and non-physical realms. These two planes exist simultaneously, each shaping reality in its own way.

The non-physical world is infinite; time does not exist, and all possibilities lie within this field. The physical world, on the other hand, is the tangible expression of what we create from the non-physical - through our thinking, vibration, and belief system.

"As above, so below. As within, so without. As the universe, so the soul."
- Hermes Trismegistus

This law of duality is demonstrated through the teaching in this ancient wisdom. As you think above, so you shall have below. As you are in the non-physical, you shall create in the physical world. As you are within yourself, you shall experience the external world.

In other words, the changes you make in your inner world will inevitably reflect in your outer reality. Science and spirituality both affirm that around 90% of your external reality is shaped by your energy. So, as you learn to raise your vibration and master your inner world, you unlock the potential to experience the flow of abundance, love, and joy that has always been waiting for you. The reality is that the experience you have is almost entirely down to you and it is absolutely possible for you to live the life you desire.

You are simply here to master this truth, to learn how to master energy and create your external world as you desire it to be.

And that is what manifestation is: the process of transforming non-physical energy into physical reality. You are the conduit, the creator. Rather than leaving creation to chance, hope, or fear, isn't it much more joyful to create intentionally - to shape a life that reflects your deepest desires, dreams, and essence?

This thought might leave you feeling excited, full of anticipation, or perhaps a little nervous. Suddenly, the way you create your life is not left to luck or circumstance; the baton is being passed back to you. You are entirely responsible for your experience. You get to choose. You CAN have all you desire. I know this realisation can bring up mixed emotions, and that's perfectly normal. Don't worry - we'll talk through it together and explore exactly how to make your dreams happen.

CHAPTER 3

THE NEGATIVE EGO

*"The energy of the mind is the
essence of life."*
- Aristotle

Before we dive into the most important part - how to apply these principles to change your life - there's one more key concept you must understand: the role of your Negative Ego.

Your mind is a powerful tool, and understanding how it works is crucial to mastering manifestation. This brings us to another universal truth: **All is Mental**.

The entire physical reality is first created through the mind. Every experience you've ever had, every decision you've made, and every reality you've lived first existed as a thought before becoming a manifested outcome. This means that what you consistently think and believe shapes your external world.

But - and this is a BIG BUT - not all of your thoughts are helpful. In fact, some of them are downright limiting. If your mind is left unchecked, it can work against you rather than for you.

Let's talk about mental hygiene

I recently led an online programme where I spoke about the importance of mental hygiene - the practice of tending to your mind with the same care and discipline you give to your body. I used a simple metaphor:

If you only brushed your teeth once a week, your breath would be... well, pretty stinky.

It's exactly the same with your mind. If you don't clean it - if you don't pay attention to what you're feeding it, what thoughts you're reinforcing, and what beliefs you're running - your thinking is going to be a bit stinky too!

We all laughed about the phrase *stinky thinking*, but it's a powerful truth. The quality of your thoughts determines the quality of your life.

So ask yourself: Is *my thinking fresh, clear, and aligned with the life I desire? Or is my thinking a little stinky - repeating old patterns, limitations, and fears?*

Your mind is your most powerful asset. It can be your greatest ally or your biggest obstacle. The good news? You get to choose. There's a well-known Cherokee story that speaks directly to this battle within us all.

A wise grandfather sits with his grandson and shares:

"Inside each of us, there are two wolves. One wolf is dark, filled with fear, anger, resentment, self-doubt, jealousy, and lack. This wolf thrives on negativity, feeding off your insecurities and limitations, whispering to you that you're not good enough, that life is unfair, that you should be afraid."

"The other wolf is light. It is filled with love, joy, courage, peace, kindness, abundance, and faith. This wolf

knows your worth, believes in your power, and reminds you that everything you need is already within you. It sees the beauty in life and moves with trust and ease."

The grandson, eyes wide with curiosity, asks,

"But Grandfather, which wolf wins?"

The grandfather gently smiles and replies,

"The one you feed."

Let's keep it simple: think of your mind as having two parts - a higher mind and a lower mind.

Your higher mind is connected to your divine truth, creativity, and intuition. It's the part of you that dreams big and recognises your infinite potential.

Your lower mind, on the other hand, is like a storage unit filled with stories, beliefs, and patterns you've accumulated throughout your life. From the moment you were born, you've been absorbing ideas - not all of which serve you. These stories often come from past experiences, societal conditioning, or even things you overheard and accepted as truth without question.

The problem? Many of these stories are outdated, limiting, and completely misaligned with the truth of who you really are. They create invisible barriers that keep you playing small, whispering doubts into your mind, and shaping your reality based on fear rather than potential.

"Until you make the unconscious conscious, it will direct your life and you will call it fate."
- Carl Jung

When a thought is repeated enough times, it becomes a belief. And as you now know, your thoughts and beliefs shape the energy you project into the world. If your beliefs are rooted in lack, fear, or self-doubt, they direct energy in ways that create more of what you *don't* want.

This is where the Negative Ego comes in. It is the part of your lower mind that clings to limiting beliefs and works relentlessly to prove them true. Its job is to maintain the status quo, even if that means keeping you stuck in patterns of suffering.

The Negative Ego thrives on being right - even when that means reinforcing painful cycles. If you hold a belief that you're not good enough, your thoughts and energy will shape a reality that reflects this belief. You will find yourself in experiences that mirror this sense of unworthiness - whether that's struggling with money, blocking love, constantly chasing the next goal, or feeling like no matter what you achieve, it's never enough.

The Negative Ego celebrates when you remain in this cycle of self-doubt. It whispers, *See? I told you - you're not good enough.* And because the subconscious mind is always working to affirm its beliefs, you unconsciously make choices that validate this narrative. You might feel paralysed by fear when an opportunity arises, push away love before it has a chance to flourish, or spend money as fast as it comes in - without even realising that these actions stem from deep-seated programming.

The Negative Ego isn't here to sabotage you on purpose - it's simply operating from old scripts. The good news? You can rewrite those scripts. By becoming aware of these limiting beliefs and replacing them with empowering ones, you can start creating from your higher mind instead. And that is exactly what we are going to work on together - practical tools and techniques that will help you break free from old patterns, dissolve limitations, and step boldly into the life you were born to experience. This isn't about wishful thinking or hoping things will change on their own. This is about reclaiming your creative power, shifting your energy, and consciously designing your reality.

> *"The mind is everything. What you think you become."*
> - Buddha

Manifestation isn't about proving your worth - it's about embodying the energy of what you desire now. The most powerful manifestations arise from alignment, not striving.

You don't manifest your dreams by chasing them. You manifest them by becoming the person who is already living them.

How the Negative Ego Can Show Up

There are some common patterns that the Negative Ego makes manifest. Let's explore a few examples so you can reflect on whether any of them are blocking the flow in your life.

Lack of Self-Worth

Your Negative Ego loves to keep you stuck in patterns - it absolutely does not like change! Even when the change is something you deeply desire, it

clings to the comfort of the familiar. Why? Because your current reality, no matter how painful or limiting, feels "safe" to the Negative Ego. It knows the rules, the terrain, and how to navigate it. Change, on the other hand, represents uncertainty, which the ego interprets as a threat.

Here's the surprising truth: your Negative Ego would rather keep you in discomfort or suffering than risk the unknown. It's not logical, but it's how the brain works. Every time you stay stuck in those familiar thought loops, your brain releases a tiny hit of dopamine, creating an addictive cycle of thoughts and feelings. Without realising it, many of us become chemically addicted to the very patterns that hold us back.

Think about that for a moment: while part of you craves freedom, joy, and transformation, another part is terrified of change - even the positive kind. So ask yourself: *Which part of me wants to stay where I am? Which part of me is afraid of the good things I desire?*

At the root of this resistance often lies a deep lack of self-worth - a belief that you don't truly deserve what you desire. But let me remind you: *You are worthy. You've always been worthy.* The journey to overcoming the Negative Ego begins with recognising its voice, gently releasing its grip, and reclaiming the truth of who you are.

> *"You are not limited by the past unless you choose to be. Every moment is a new beginning."*
> - Unknown

Upper Limits Problem / Sabotaging Success

You might think you want to manifest everything you've ever dreamed of - and logically, why wouldn't you? But here's the kicker: there's often a part of you that *doesn't want it.*

Wait, what? I know that sounds absurd, but it's true. Your brain creates habit loops - thoughts that trigger feelings, which lead to actions, which reinforce those thoughts. If those loops are rooted in a lack of self-worth or a fear of success, your subconscious will find ways to keep you stuck.

When you start breaking out of these patterns, your subconscious panics. It feels unfamiliar and unsafe, even if the new path is good for you. To protect itself, your Negative Ego triggers a negative thought, which leads to self-sabotaging behaviour.

Here's where it gets tricky: when you fall back into the old pattern, your brain rewards you with a tiny dopamine hit. That reward reinforces the cycle, and before you know it, you're back where you started.

Humans can literally become addicted to their own cycles of suffering. It's not because we want to stay stuck; it's because the brain craves the safety of the known - even if it's painful.

Take a moment to reflect:

- Are there cycles or patterns of thinking you keep returning to?

- Is there something in your life you've always wanted to achieve but haven't quite reached?

- Where might you be holding yourself back for fear of change or success?

These questions may feel uncomfortable, but awareness is the first step to healing. Getting honest with yourself about where you're stuck will pave the way for growth, freedom, and the life you truly desire.

Fear: The Silent Architect of Limitation

"Fear is the cheapest room in the house. I would like to see you living in better conditions."
- Hafiz

Fear is one of the greatest forces that keeps us stuck. Fear of success, fear of failure, fear of judgement, fear of what others might think - these fears act as invisible chains, holding us back from stepping into our full potential. And the truth is, your Negative Ego thrives on fear. Fear is its language, its playground, its weapon of choice.

Whether it's fear of losing what you have, fear of the unknown, or fear of being seen and judged, the Negative Ego uses these worries to keep you small. It pulls you into cycles of overthinking, clinging to the past, and catastrophising about the future. It distracts you from the one place where your true power resides: the present moment.

The present moment is where all possibilities exist. It's where you access clarity, creativity, and connection to your higher self. But fear's goal is to keep you away from this power. It scatters your focus, leaving you chasing shadows - problems that don't yet exist or pains you've already survived. And here's the thing: *What you focus your energy upon grows.* So, as you let fear pull you out of stillness and presence, you're inadvertently creating more of the same fearful, limited experiences.

But what if I told you that fear isn't real? Fear is, quite literally, False Evidence Appearing Real. It's the mind weaving stories from what *might* happen, creating an illusion so convincing that you react to it as though it's the truth. It feels real, but it's not the truth of who you are or what's possible for you.

> "Everything you've ever wanted is
> on the other side of fear."
> - George Addair

Fear of not being good enough, a lack of self-worth, and a fear of success are some of the most powerful blocks preventing you from living a life of bliss, joy, and abundance. These fears become invisible walls, quietly standing between you and your dreams.

These patterns can manifest in many ways, often without you even realising it. Here are some examples of how they might be showing up in your life:

- Spending time with people you know you need to let go of, clinging to relationships that no longer serve your growth.

- Saying yes when your heart knows you need to say no.

- Playing the blame game - projecting your suffering or fears onto others and making your struggles their fault.

- Gossiping or speaking negatively about others as a way to deflect from your own inner discomfort.

- Struggling with inaction - not taking any steps toward the change you deeply desire.

- Chasing one goal after another, always striving for the "next level" but never feeling safe, content, or grateful for what you already have.

- People-pleasing and constantly worrying about how others perceive you, letting their opinions hold you hostage.

- Neglecting self-care, putting yourself at the very bottom of your priority list while rushing to take care of everyone else.

"Fear does not prevent death.
It prevents life."
- Naguib Mahfouz

These patterns keep you stuck in a cycle that feels exhausting and unfulfilling. But here's the truth: these behaviours are not a reflection of who you truly are. They are the whispers of fear and unworthiness, holding you back from stepping into your full power. And that is what manifestation is: a path of empowerment. It is realising what you are capable of, quitting the limiting stories, stepping into your power and saying - "I desire it and therefore I shall create it. I expect great things, I expect miracles."

The moment you begin to recognise and release these old patterns, you open yourself up to the freedom, ease, and abundance that has always been waiting for you. It starts with awareness. It starts with you.

It's vital for you to know this: you are worthy and deserving of everything you desire. If it wasn't meant for you, you wouldn't feel the pull toward it. Nothing is impossible for the infinite, divine reality in which you live - absolutely nothing.

It's time to come home to the truth that you deserve to experience a life more magnificent than you can imagine. I want you to live a "pinch me, is this real?" kind of life. While everything I share with you is grounded in truth and reality, the first step is knowing, in your heart, that you deserve to make these changes. Because you do.

*"You were born with wings. Why
prefer to crawl through life?"*
- Rumi

CHAPTER 4

MANIFESTING WHAT YOU DO WANT & THE 'WHEN I' PARADOX

"Act as if what you intend to manifest is already true. The universe will respond accordingly."
- Dr. Joe Dispenza

You are manifesting all the time - not just some of the time. Energy is constantly flowing through you, and your life is a continual manifestation of the frequency and vibration you are expressing. Your thoughts, emotions, and actions shape your vibration, and the life you experience is a direct reflection of the resonance at which you're vibrating.

Let's simplify this with an example.

Imagine you wake up in the morning feeling tired and grumpy because you hit snooze too many times. You realise you're running late, and as you jump out of bed, you stub your toe (or perhaps step on an unpleasant "gift" from the cat!). You rush through your morning, barely present, your mind swirling with worries and fears. You dwell on how much you dislike your job and how you'd rather not go to work. Outside, it's raining and grey, which only deepens your sense of dread and frustration. You scroll the news and see more awful things happening in the world. You're so caught up in the chaos of your own thoughts that you fail to notice any beauty or joy around you.

As you carry this low vibration into your day, you'll naturally attract experiences that match it. The barista at the coffee shop is short-tempered - perhaps they're having a bad morning too. At work, you encounter difficult colleagues, challenging emails, and tense meetings. By the end of the day, you're exhausted and uninspired, only to repeat the same cycle again tomorrow. Life feels like a constant grind, devoid of joy or fulfilment.

Now, let's consider a different scenario.

You wake up feeling refreshed because you went to bed early. You have time to meditate, exercise, or engage in practices that raise your vibration. You start your day by focusing on gratitude - taking a moment to appreciate the things in your life that bring you joy, from the warmth of your bed to the opportunity to create a new day. Instead of rushing, you move through your morning with intention and presence, perhaps enjoying a healthy breakfast or a few quiet moments to connect with your breath.

As you carry this higher vibration into your day, the world begins to respond differently. The barista greets you with a warm smile, work interactions flow effortlessly, and solutions to challenges seem to arise naturally. You notice small moments of beauty - a stranger's smile, the sparkle of rain on the pavement, or the kindness of someone holding the door open. Your day unfolds with ease, peace, and flow. By the time you settle in for the evening, you feel fulfilled, aligned, and energised - ready to create another meaningful day tomorrow.

Here's the truth:

**These days don't happen by luck.
Amazing lives don't happen by luck.
They happen through you.**

One of the greatest myths about manifestation is that it's all about "big things" - the dream home, the lottery win, the life filled with love, joy, and abundance. But here's the catch: if you're constantly wanting those things, hoping they'll come to change your life, you're missing the point. Manifestation doesn't respond to what you want in the future. It responds to the energy you're embodying right now.

And this is where the 'When I' paradox comes in.

It sounds like this:

- "When I get the job, then I'll feel successful."

- "When I find the right relationship, then I'll feel complete."

- "When I make more money, then I'll finally relax."

The assumption is that external achievements or circumstances will unlock the inner peace and fulfilment you long for. So you chase, you strive, you wait - convinced that those who already have what you desire must have reached some secret state of wholeness.

But here's the paradox: this very belief - this waiting to feel whole - creates the exact block that keeps what you desire out of reach. When you tell yourself that happiness, confidence, or peace will come *after* you achieve something, you send a powerful signal to the Universe: *I don't have it now.* And because energy responds to your current vibration, you continue to manifest the experience of *not having it.*

The truth? You must first embody the energy of what you desire.

You don't attract success by proving you are worthy of it; you attract success by knowing you already are.

The shift is subtle, but it changes everything:

- "When I feel successful, the opportunities will flow."

- "When I love myself, the right relationship will arrive."

- "When I relax and trust, abundance will naturally expand."

You manifest your greatest dreams through becoming first.

This is why so many people say they want to win the lottery, but in reality, they are only affirming lack. "When I win the lottery, then I can finally live the life I want." But you are manifesting from the now. If your current energy is, "I need to win the lottery so I can fulfil my dreams," then what you are really broadcasting is, "I do not have enough now. I am not abundant now."

And energy doesn't lie.

The odds of winning the lottery are astronomical - between 1 in 50 million and 1 in 100 million. Statistically, you are:

- More likely to be struck by lightning (1 in 1 million per year in the UK).

- More likely to be attacked by a shark (1 in 3.7 million globally).

- Far more likely to become a millionaire through entrepreneurship (1 in 25 for business owners in the UK).

Not only that, but many who *do* win the lottery end up losing their fortune within a few years. Why? Because their internal energy never changed. They still lived in scarcity, so they unconsciously recreated scarcity. You manifest your greatest dreams by becoming first - so that when the big things arrive, you can hold them with ease, knowing you are worthy of them.

This is where many people go wrong with manifestation. They repeat affirmations, visualise their desires, and then wait - expecting the big things to just appear. But they miss a crucial step.

Big things don't just land out of nowhere. They are built on small, consistent shifts.

Affirmations, visualisation, and all the tools we're about to dive into will work - but only when you use them to change how you feel now, in this moment. That's the real key.

Over time, as your internal state shifts, life will begin to flow with greater ease. Big manifestations don't start with grand gestures; they start with small moments of gratitude, practiced day by day.

"You do not attract what you want.
You attract what you are."
- Dr. Wayne Dyer

CHAPTER 5

BRIDGING THE GAP BETWEEN WHERE YOU ARE AND WHERE YOU WANT TO BE

*"Happiness is not something
ready - made. It comes from your
own actions."*
- Dalai Lama

Living in a state of *'When I'* creates an energetic gap between where you are and where you want to be. And this is where most of the human race is stuck - wishing, hoping, and believing their deepest desires exist somewhere in the future.

The next big thing. The next goal. The next career rung. The next great love. The higher salary.

But in chasing what's next, they miss the most powerful moment of all - the now.

And the greater the gap, the harder it feels to reach those desires, because the energy of longing is the energy of separation.

Here's where it gets really interesting. That gap isn't just metaphorical - it has a measurable frequency.

We've already established that everything is energy, including your emotions. Emotion quite literally means *energy in motion* - it is the vibrational response of your inner being to your thoughts, beliefs, and experiences. Every emotion you feel carries a unique frequency, radiating into the energetic field around you and influencing the way the world responds to you.

This is why your emotions are so powerful - they shape your internal reality and determine the external reality you create.

The groundbreaking work of Dr. David R. Hawkins, particularly in his book *Power vs. Force*, mapped out the vibrational frequency of emotions on a scale from 0 to 1,000. His research demonstrated that certain emotional states expand and elevate your energy, while others contract and restrict it.

When you embody high-frequency emotions like love, joy, and gratitude, your energy flows in alignment with creation - the non-physical world of the divine and infinite universe. You radiate abundance, ease, and expansion, making it effortless to attract experiences that match that vibration.

However, when you dwell in low-frequency emotions like fear, shame, or guilt, your energy contracts. Your perception narrows, and the external world reflects that limitation back to you - creating more experiences that affirm those lower states. Here's how emotional frequencies rank, from highest to lowest:

High-Frequency Emotions
(Expansive, Empowering States)

- **Enlightenment (700 - 1,000)** – Pure consciousness, connection with the Divine, total peace.

- **Peace (600)** – Transcendence of duality, a state of serenity and oneness.

- **Joy (540)** – Inner harmony, unconditional love, and deep bliss.

- **Love (500)** – Unconditional compassion, connection, and kindness.

- **Reason (400)** – Intellectual clarity, understanding, and wisdom.

- **Acceptance (350)** – Trusting and embracing life as it is, free from resistance.

- **Willingness (310)** – Openness to growth, constructive energy, optimism.

Mid-Frequency Emotions
(Transition States)

- **Neutrality (250)** – Feeling safe, calm, and unattached.

- **Courage (200)** – Taking responsibility, stepping into empowerment, and facing life with strength.

Low-Frequency Emotions
(Contractive, Draining States)

- **Pride (175)** – Over-identification with the ego, attachment to status.

- **Anger (150)** – Frustration, blame, and resistance to circumstances.

- **Desire (125)** – Craving and attachment to external outcomes.

- **Fear (100)** – Anxiety, worry, and a sense of powerlessness.

- **Grief (75)** – Sorrow, loss, and regret.

- **Apathy (50)** – A sense of hopelessness, indifference, and disconnection.

- **Guilt (30)** – Self-recrimination and feelings of inadequacy.

- **Shame (20)** – The lowest frequency, tied to humiliation and self-rejection.

"Success is not to be pursued;
it is to be attracted by the person
you become."
- Jim Rohn

How This Relates to Manifestation

"Seek not to change the world, but choose to change your mind about the world."
- A Course in Miracles

If you are vibrating in a state of lack, frustration, or fear, you are energetically affirming that you don't have what you want. And because the universe mirrors your frequency back to you, you continue to experience more lack, more frustration, and more fear.

This is why the 'When I' paradox is so dangerous. It keeps you locked in lower vibrational states - in longing, in separation, in the belief that happiness exists somewhere else, sometime later.

Think about how these energies show up in your life.

- What is the quality of your thinking?

- Are you living in fear and frustration?

- Do you spend time dwelling on when things have gone wrong, worrying about the future, or trying to figure out how to make what you want happen?

Now, look at the things in your life that you wish were different.

- What is the energy you hold around them?

- Do you spend most of your time focusing on what you don't like about your current situation?

- Does that focus pull you into a lower frequency?

- Or are you holding the energy of the outcome you desire?

Most people are surprised that courage is not higher on the scale. But think about it - courage is not a deep knowing. Courage is about finding the strength to overcome something, and while it is a shift out of lower frequencies, it still carries resistance.

The Emotional State You Need to Manifest

"Abundance is not something we acquire. It is something we tune into."
- Wayne Dyer

What we want is for you to reach a place of absolute love. A state of absolute knowing that the things you desire will happen.

You don't need to know how they will happen. You don't need to know when they will happen.

You just trust they will. You trust that things are working out for you rather than not.

And you live in that energy.

When you reach that emotional resonance, it is impossible for the things you desire not to occur.

So, your entire job is to focus on how you feel in this present moment.

To live and act as if it is already done.

This is your number one priority. I want to show you an example of how what we expect shapes what we experience.

The other day, I was in London, and before I even stepped off the train, I set my intention: "I expect miracles today."

As I walked through the station, I let myself notice the good - the warmth in people's faces, small gestures of kindness, the hum of life moving in harmony. I smiled, repeating my mantra: "I believe in miracles."

Before getting on the tube, I stopped for what I like to call a hug in a mug - a warm drink to carry me through the morning. As I reached for my purse, the woman behind the counter looked at me and said, "I would like to gift you this."

It was such a simple moment, yet profoundly affirming.

Einstein once said, "The most important decision we make is whether we believe we live in a friendly or a hostile universe."

Most people unconsciously expect struggle before ease, obstacles before opportunities. But when we expect good things, good things happen.

This wasn't about getting a free coffee - it was about the energy I chose to hold. When we shift our expectations from fear to trust, from doubt to possibility, life mirrors that shift back to us.

The universe is always listening, always responding. Can you see that this is what manifestation truly is?

It's not just about the big things - it's about flowing energy, finding beauty in the simple moments, and allowing those small, everyday experiences to build upon one another.

When you choose to see life through this lens, every exchange, every act of kindness, every moment of gratitude becomes part of something greater. These moments don't just add up - they expand, creating a life filled with more ease, more joy, more miracles.

The question is, what are you expecting?

Mastering Your Mind & The Power of Healing in Manifestation

While you are here on Earth, having a physical experience, you will encounter your Negative Ego - that relentless voice of doubt, fear, and limitation. The work, then, is about consciously rising above this chatter and intentionally shifting your focus toward higher possibilities.

We've already explored how all emotions carry a frequency - and that the longer you dwell on a negative thought, the more similar thoughts you attract. Like a magnet, your energy field begins to draw in experiences that match your dominant vibration.

This is why mastering your thoughts is paramount. The more time you spend thinking expansively, considering what is truly possible beyond the conditioning of your past, the more your reality shifts. Over time, your thoughts shape your beliefs, and your beliefs become the foundation of your physical world.

All thought turns to form. So the most important work you can do is to make sure that your thinking is constructive, powerful, and infused with grand possibility.

Here's where healing comes into play. Manifestation isn't just about thinking positively - it's about clearing the internal blocks that keep you stuck in cycles of doubt and limitation.

The egoic mind seeks validation from the external world, attaching itself to outcomes, past wounds, and limiting beliefs. To truly rise above this, healing must happen from within.

While talk therapy can be helpful to a point, it often keeps you circling the same thoughts. If the mind created the problem, staying in the mind won't solve it. This is why so many people spend years in therapy (sometimes decades!) yet still feel stuck. I've worked with countless clients who came to me after 25+ years in therapy, finally ready to try something different - to go deeper than the programming of the mind itself.

This is where energy healing becomes so powerful. Unlike traditional approaches, it works beyond the mental level, reaching the energetic structures that hold these limitations in place. I've witnessed miracles through the Mystery School healings and ancient modalities of the lineage of King Salomon - profound shifts that clear, rewire, and elevate a person's entire vibrational state.

If you are truly serious about manifestation and stepping into the highest version of yourself, clearing your energy field is non-negotiable.

Manifestation is about flipping your focus - no longer reacting to what is happening in your outer world as the measure of how you feel, but instead recognising that your inner state is what creates your reality.

Your inner world is everything. When you shift your attention away from the external and dedicate yourself fully to raising your vibration, clearing your energy, and aligning with higher frequencies, your outer world will transform as a reflection of that internal shift.

This is true empowerment - the recognition that you have the power to change everything in your world.

So how do you shift? You align yourself with the frequency of the life you want now. You embody the energy of joy, gratitude, and abundance before the external world reflects it back to you.

You stop waiting for the external to change so you can feel better, and you start feeling better so the external can change.

This is self-mastery. This is manifestation.

And in the second half of the book we are going to delve into the exact steps to make this happen.

Now that you have the pieces of the puzzle - the fact it is all energy and that it is you who is the projector of that energy into the physical world - let's talk about how you can manifest what you DO want in your life rather than what you don't.

This leads us to self-love - the foundation of everything.

The single most important key to living in alignment with the greatest version of yourself is recognising that you deserve it. YOU DO.

You deserve to have your dreams come true.

You deserve peace.

You deserve joy.

You deserve freedom.

You deserve abundance.

And you do not need to feel guilty for wanting more. You do not need to believe that life has to be a struggle.

You are worthy - right now.

Yes, you may need to take risks. Yes, you may have to do deep inner work. Yes, you may have to show up for yourself in ways you never have before.

But you are worthy of it all.

And here's the truth - it is entirely possible for you.

Most people spend their lives chasing worthiness - believing that the next achievement, the next person's approval, or the next milestone will finally make them enough. They live in a constant loop of seeking validation, never realising that their worth was never in question to begin with.

But manifestation doesn't work from this energy.

Can you see why loving yourself is so essential? It really is the master key.

You must already know you are loveable. You must already know you are enough. You must recognise that the only validation that truly matters is your own.

You Are a Miracle

There will never be another you.

No one else will ever walk this Earth with your exact essence. No one with your laugh. No one with your smile. No one with your frequency, your purpose, your reason for being here.

You are a miracle.

And it is time for you to believe that. It is time for you to own that. It is time for you to put the negative self-chat down and start believing in what could be possible! It is time for you to become your own greatest champion.

Because when you do - everything changes.

What becomes possible when you start living with a mindset of manifestation?

Honestly? Anything.

You are supposed to have great health. You are supposed to experience abundance, love, joy, and ease - because these are your birthright.

I describe living in alignment as being in the "green light zone."

Things just flow.

And when you start raising your frequency, shifting your thoughts, and applying the tools I'm about to share, you will notice something - the world around you begins to respond differently.

At first, it will be the small things.

You'll find yourself hitting every green light on your drive. You'll breeze through tasks that used to frustrate you. The barista gifts you a coffee.

A stranger offers to help you. Your manager unexpectedly gives you a day off in recognition of your work. A new client appears. An idea lands effortlessly in your mind - something that you used to strain for. You wake up with more energy, feeling lighter, happier. You start noticing the magic in the ordinary - the softness of morning light, the laughter of a stranger, the feeling of gratitude for the laundry because it means you have clothes to wash.

This is how it begins.

The days that used to feel "just okay" start to feel better.

And as you continue to make your vibration your number one priority, the energy builds.

Your relationships deepen. New, aligned people start showing up in your life in the most unexpected ways. Surprises happen - money you weren't expecting, opportunities that seem to come from nowhere, shifts that make life so much easier. Your confidence rises. You finally take the leap you've been holding back on.

And then - the bigger things begin to manifest.

A new job. A thriving business. An effortless flow of money. Work that feels like your soul's purpose. Feeling strong, radiant, and deeply at home in your body. The relationship you've always dreamed of - or a complete transformation in the one you already have. A bank balance that keeps growing.

Because this is how it works.

It starts small, but as you continue to align, trust, and raise your frequency, the momentum becomes unstoppable.

And once you enter this flow, everything changes.

Now it is your turn…

"Don't wait for a miracle.
Be the miracle."
- Unknown

Let's begin with the most important question you will ever ask yourself:

Who are you?

This is a question I hope you return to for the rest of your life. Because you are not your name. You are not your job. You are not the roles you play - mother, wife, sister, friend. These are expressions of you, but they are not you.

Who you are cannot be defined in words alone, because you are so much more than an identity.

Before you came into this physical reality, you chose your path. You weren't randomly placed here - you made agreements, sacred contracts for your soul's evolution that reside in the Akashic field, woven into the fabric of your being. Even your astrological birth chart holds keys to your mission - the lessons you came here to learn, the gifts you came here to share.

And this is why I need you to own just how much you matter.

You need to let go of the self-doubt, the fear, the limitation, the worry, and the focus on lack, because all of it is keeping you trapped in the very patterns you are trying to break free from. Every time you tell yourself the same old story, you reinforce it. Every time you hold back your light, you deny yourself and the world the truth of who you are.

You have been expecting small and not good enough for too long.

It is time to step forward. To stop waiting. To stop playing small.

You were never meant to shrink yourself to fit into the physical world - you are here to be the light being you are, to expand and create. To embody the highest expression of who you are and your divinity. The truth is, your energy doesn't just affect you. It ripples out into the collective. Your healing, your growth, your rise in vibration doesn't happen in isolation - it shifts the entire field of all of us.

This is why you must let go of the old idea that putting yourself first is selfish. It is the opposite. Service to self is service to the whole.

You cannot give what you do not have. You cannot lift others if you are weighed down. You cannot lead if you are lost in self-doubt. The more you rise, the greater your impact will be. So know this. It is safe for you to desire greater things. It is safe for you to be you in the world. It is in fact exactly what we need: you weaving your divine frequency through the fabric of the entire human collective.

The fact that you are here, reading this, is not a coincidence. You have a mission. You have been calling in change, asking for clarity, asking for a way forward. And now the answers are in front of you.

The only question is - will you step through the door and claim what is possible for you?

It's all about JOY!

*"There is no way to happiness -
happiness is the way."*
- Thich Nhat Hanh

Now that you understand vibration - and the danger of the 'When I' paradigm - you also understand that the work to transform your reality is not outside of you. It's within.

Your external world is a mirror, reflecting the energy, thoughts, and beliefs you hold inside.

You are that powerful.

You are always creating your reality.

And now, you also know this: every possible version of your life already exists in the quantum field.

Your only job? To match the vibration of the reality you desire so that it can materialise into your external world.

But before we go any further, I want you to know something deeply important.

The reason you want what you want - the dream home, the money, the success, the love, the body, the freedom - is because you believe it will bring you joy.

And here's the truth:

It won't.

Nothing external to you creates joy.

Joy is an inside job. It's something you cultivate, something you generate from within.

Think about it.

How many people do you know - or at least know of - who have everything they once wished for, yet they are still not happy? The house, the wealth, the fame, the body, the partner - yet something still feels empty.

Stuff does not make you happy.

You just think it will.

And when you finally get what you thought you wanted, you won't feel much different - because the mind will immediately move on to the next thing. Another goal, another achievement, another level of desire.

This is why 95% of lottery winners are worse off a year after winning than they were before. They thought money would fix everything. But without doing the inner work, they weren't prepared to hold or sustain the life they suddenly had.

If you don't do the inner work, you won't be able to retain the things you receive.

For a tree to grow strong, it needs the right conditions - rich, fertile soil, deep roots, and care at the foundation level.

The healthier the roots, the greater the tree's capacity to flourish and bear fruit.

But when it comes to manifestation, most people focus only on the fruit - the external results. They forget about the roots.

Without deep roots, a tree cannot stand.

Without deep inner work, manifestations cannot last.

So here's the biggest secret to manifestation:

It's not about the stuff.

It's about joy.

When you shift your focus to feeling joy now - not someday, not when you reach the next level, but right now - you make it impossible for what you desire not to come to you.

Because, my love, you have just matched the frequency of the Universe.

Joy is the frequency of the Universe.

When you become joy within, you allow everything else to unfold around you.

This is the truth most people miss. And now that you see it, everything changes.

Embodying the feeling of your desires

If you woke up tomorrow in your dream life, what would it feel like?

Not just what would be happening, but how would you experience it?

- Want the dream home? Close your eyes - what does it feel like to wake up in that space? To move through it, to breathe it in, to know it's yours?

- Want a body that feels strong, light, and full of energy? What does it feel like to live inside it every single day?

- Want greater abundance? What does it feel like to have money flow to you effortlessly, to know that there is always more than enough?

This is the shift you must make.

Moving forward, you are going to have to fight for your energy.

You will have to pull yourself - again and again - out of the lower vibrational version of you. The one who is still waiting. The one who is stuck in the 'When I' paradigm, believing that joy is something you will feel later, after the manifestation of what you want.

Because the truth is, you must become the person you want to be now. Become who they are within and it is impossible for your life not to transform without. You really don't need to worry about the external or the how. All you need is to focus all your energy on what it would feel like to have the things you want and to take aligned action from that place.

The version of you who already has those things - the person who is living that life - they feel it first.

The greatest version of you holds the energy before the physical proof arrives.

That's the work. That's the shift.

And the moment you claim it, everything starts to move.

Life is not happening to you. You are happening to life. Life is happening through you: your beliefs, your projection, your vibration.

This world is a school, and you are here to master it - to step into your power, to align with your highest truth, and to learn how to shape reality in a way that honours your deepest desires.

Let's begin. Let's take these teachings off the page and into your life.

"The world is a mirror, forever reflecting what you are thinking, feeling, and believing."
- Neville Goddard

CHAPTER 6

MANIFESTING IN THE SIMPLEST OF STEPS

Manifestation doesn't have to be complicated. At its core, it follows a simple rhythm - one that, when understood and embodied, changes everything.

Before we dive into the details, let's start with the four foundational steps that make manifestation work at the highest level.

Step 1: Imagine

The first step is to *imagine* what you truly want. Not just in vague ideas, but in vivid, undeniable detail. If it's a dream home - where is it? Walk through it in your mind. Notice the colours, the textures, the light streaming through the windows. Feel the warmth of the space. The same applies to anything else you desire - wealth, love, freedom. Get clear on what it looks like, sounds like, feels like. Write it down, make it real.

Step 2: Feel the Feeling

The second step is to FEEL the energy of your dream as if it is already yours. What would that feel like in your body? Would you breathe easier? Would you feel light, expansive, free? What does wealth feel like - not just in numbers, but as a deep sense of ease and possibility? What does love feel like in every cell of your being? Step into that feeling NOW.

Step 3: Let Go & Trust

The moment you start asking, 'How will it happen? Why isn't it here yet?' you've stepped out of flow and into resistance. Your mind loves control, but manifestation doesn't work that way. Step three is about surrender. Trust the process. Let go of the timeline. Keep your focus on the feeling of it already being done, and act as if.

Step 4: Patience, Belief & Practice

The final step is patience, belief, and practice. Holding a high vibration takes commitment - it's a daily practice of choosing trust over doubt, belief over fear. Your mind will try to pull you down, but you are stronger than that. Keep returning to these tools, keep anchoring in the feeling of your dream being real. Miracles happen all the time - why not for you? The Universe *wants* to conspire in your favour, but you must be open to receiving it.

These four steps are the foundation of manifestation. Now, let's go deeper - let's make it happen for you.

Stepping into action

Throughout the rest of this book, you'll see some of the same words popping up over and over. As we move through the rest of this material together, I am going to keep repeating the following affirmation because I want you to keep saying these words, over and over again. I want you to OWN this reality. Get these following statements scripted into your mind and repeat them on loop - don't simply think them, FEEL them and own them. Shout them when you are out running; sing them in the shower. Programme them into the depths of your psyche. This is the new you.

I am love. I am light. I am powerful. I am a creator. I am here to create my experience.

So, here's your step-by-step action plan to make that happen.

Because here's something else you need to know - manifestation isn't just about shifting your inner game.

Yes, your thoughts, beliefs, and energy create your reality, but that alone isn't enough.

You also have to take action.

Not just any action - aligned, intentional, often uncomfortable action.

If you want a different life, you must do things differently.

You cannot create new results while repeating the same patterns.

As our great friend Albert Einstein famously said, *"Insanity is doing the same thing over and over again and expecting different results."*

And that's exactly what most people do.

They dream, they visualise, they hope - but they never step beyond what feels safe.

This is where the real work begins.

Transformation isn't just about what you think - it's about what you do.

At this point, you understand energy, vibration, and the truth that you are always manifesting.

But knowing this isn't enough - you have to LIVE it.

And that's where most people get stuck.

They understand the concepts, but they don't have a clear system to apply them daily.

That's why I created the **CREATE** Method.

This is your step-by-step guide to shifting your energy, taking aligned action, and making manifestation a way of life.

No more guessing.

No more wondering why it's not working.

With CREATE, you will always know where you are and how to move forward.

So without further ado, we will now focus the rest of our time together on how you CREATE your new reality.

C - Clarity & Commitment

If you want to get somewhere, you need to know where you're going. You don't just jump in your car and drive aimlessly - you set a destination.

Manifestation works the same way. Energy follows intention. If you don't have clarity on what you want, how can life bring it to you?

The first step is getting clear. And for many people, this is where the real work begins - because when they ask themselves, *"What do I actually want?"* they don't know. So before anything else, you have to create that vision.

Then comes commitment.

If you want something different, you have to fight for it. Now that you understand the nature of your mind - that you have a negative ego and a lower self that prefers to stay stuck - you must actively choose to act against that resistance.

You have to commit to actions that might feel un-comfortable at first (and eventually, they'll become your favourite part of life). You have to commit to better habits, to raising your vibration, to aligning your ener-gy and focus. Every choice you make - how you care for yourself, how you spend your time, how you direct your thoughts - it all matters.

Because what you want?

It's on the other side of everything you've been avoiding.

R - Raise Your Frequency

Your vibration is everything - because it's what shapes your reality.

From this moment forward, how you feel becomes your highest priority. You must build awareness around your energy at all times. How you think, what you say, who you spend time with, how you wake up, how you nourish your body, what you eat - it all matters because it is all vibrational. This is about more than just feeling good. This is where the deeper work needs to happen. This is where you are going to have to review what you believe about yourself and about life. It's about intentionally creating habits, rituals, and practices that elevate your frequency so that you become a vibrational match for the life you desire.

Because when you feel good, you don't just experience life differently - you attract better, you create better, and you manifest effortlessly.

E - Embody the Energy

Manifestation isn't about *getting* **- it's about being.**

You don't wait for love to feel loved. You don't wait for wealth to feel abundant. You don't wait for success to feel worthy. You become the energy of it now.

This step is about identity - shifting your internal world first. When you embody the energy of your desires, the external must adjust to match you. Thinking about what you want and desire (rather than what you don't) is asking the universe for what you want. Feeling the feelings (right now) of what it will be when it is done is what will bring it to you. In a world where everything is about DOING, this step represents a paradigm shift. This step is about BEING. It's about learning to trust that the universe is creating with you, that the universe is good, and that good things can happen. This is where you learn to expect miracles.

A - Act from Alignment

Once you have learned to raise your frequency, shift your focus to how you feel, and trust from a place of being, then - and only then - it's time to take action.

But not just any action.

Aligned action comes from love, not fear. It comes from expecting great things to happen instead of reacting to life from a place of survival.

Imagine moving through the world, trusting fully that life is unfolding in your favour. What kind of action would you take if you knew, without a doubt, that things were working out for you?

Manifestation is co-creation.

The universe cannot meet you where you are if you don't move first. When you take inspired action, you open the doors for the universe to flow in and support you in ways you could never predict.

But here's where most people get stuck: fear.

If you want a bigger life, you're going to have to take bold steps that stretch you beyond your comfort zone. And this is where the ego will try to pull you back - convincing you that staying small is safe.

This is why we resist the very things that will bring us the most joy - because the greatest fear humans have is not who they are now, but who they could become.

If you want to step into a bigger life, you have to take the leap.

You don't wait for it to happen. You make it happen.

T - Trust Your Inner Wisdom

Trust has an entire place in this acronym because it is everything.

You must learn to trust that things are working out for you, even when you can't see how. You must trust your inner wisdom, your intuition, and the quiet knowing within you - rather than the fear-based chatter of your mind.

Overcoming the fear, programming, and limitations of the negative ego is one of the most important things you will ever do. And to do that, you must learn to trust in the unseen, trust in yourself, and trust that far bigger things are possible for you than you've ever allowed yourself to believe. Einstein said that one of the first things that human beings need to ask themselves is whether the universe is friendly or hostile.

If you don't trust in a good universe, then you are acting from a state of survival. You HAVE to get into the mindset that things are working out FOR you, not against you. Trust it will happen and let it go.

E - Expand Beyond Limits

As above, so below. As within, so without.

The bigger you think, the bigger you create. Your job is to learn how to draw infinite energy from the non-physical into your physical world, shaping your reality in ways beyond what you've ever imagined. This is how you create your own Camelot - your dream life, built from the inside out.

Right now, you might only be creating at 3% of your full capacity - and look at what you've already achieved!

So the real question is: what else is possible for you?

This is where everything comes together. You apply all the previous steps, and then you go beyond. You stretch yourself. You expand your vision. You think far bigger than you ever have before.

Because if you think big, your magick will be big. And if you think small - well, you already know what to expect.

In the end, it is, and always has been, you who creates your reality. The CREATE framework is designed to guide you through the key stages of manifestation - again and again, bringing you back to your power.

Like any journey, it all begins with knowing where you're going. Each step builds upon the last, helping you understand not just how to manifest, but why you may have struggled in the past.

As you move through this process, you'll start to see the exact places where you get stuck - and, more importantly, how to move beyond them.

Let's now start applying this wisdom through some specific techniques, so that you can create massive transformation and step into your divine birthright.

CHAPTER 7

CLARITY AND COMMITMENT

I am love. I am light. I am powerful.
I am a creator. I am here to create
my experience.

Before you can create anything, you must first have clarity. Just as a traveller wouldn't set off without a destination in mind, you can't manifest what you desire without first defining it.

The clearer you are about what you truly want, the easier it becomes to align your energy, take inspired action, and allow it to unfold.

And yet, this is often where people get stuck. When given absolute freedom to define what they want, they feel overwhelmed, uncertain, even paralysed by the endless possibilities.

The human mind is often far better at recognising what it doesn't want than clearly articulating what it does. It fixates on past struggles, limitations, and fears, spending so much time focused on what's wrong that it unknowingly reinforces it.

But as you now know, what you focus on expands. If your attention stays on what you don't want, you will inevitably create more of it.

This is why clarity is essential. Defining what you want - not just vaguely, but in vivid detail - shifts your energy, your focus, and ultimately, your reality. Clarity is important, but commitment is EVERYTHING. Knowing what you want isn't enough - you must DECIDE. Fully, wholeheartedly, without hesitation. You must **commit to the next and greatest version of yourself**, refusing to waver, refusing to settle. Without commitment, manifestation remains a dream. But the moment you commit, the Universe starts rearranging everything in your favour.

This is where you step up. Where you declare: *I am ready. I choose this. I will not turn back.*

Because if you are not truly committed, it isn't going to happen. You must decide that you are no longer available for limitation, for playing small, for tolerating anything less than what you know you are meant for. Where there is a WILL, there is always a way.

This is your moment to commit - not just in words, but in action. To the version of you who already has it. To making the hard but right decisions. To facing your fears. To stepping into discomfort and doing what must be done.

It is time for you to rise. To become the spiritual WARRIOR you were always meant to be. To stop holding yourself back.

You ready, sister? Let's do this.

Action Step: Invest in a Journal

I am love. I am light. I am powerful. I am a creator. I am here to create my experience. Your transformation begins now.

And it starts with a simple but powerful act - getting yourself a brand-new journal, one that brings you joy.

Yes, your first step is to treat yourself.

Choose one that feels special, one that excites you when you open it every day.

Because this journal is about to become the space where you write your new reality into existence.

Personally, I like a lot of space, so I always tend to choose an A4 journal - but you must choose whatever feels good to you.

Action Step: Questioning and Visioning

Now that you have your journal, it's time to get clear.

Clarity begins with asking better questions.

So take a deep breath, drop into this moment, and allow yourself to imagine freely - without limitation, without restriction.

If you woke up tomorrow, and everything in your life was like you were living in a dream - what would be happening?

If there were no limitations, what would your dream life look like? What would be happening? Who would you be?

Go deep. Imagine each area of your life:

- Your body - How does it feel to live in a body that is strong, healthy, and vibrant?

- Your relationships - What kind of love, connection, and support surrounds you?

- Your family - What is the energy in your home? How do you show up for each other?

- Your finances - How does it feel to have total financial freedom? What choices would you make?

- Your community - What impact do you have on the world around you? How do you serve?

- Your home - What kind of space do you wake up in every day?

- Your career - What work excites you? How do you express your gifts? Take your time with this. Sit with it. What do you truly want? Not what you think you *should* want. Not what feels *realistic*. Not what others might *approve of*.

Strip away the doubt, the "how would I even make that happen?" and the "what will people think?"

If there were no limits - what would you desire, fully and unapologetically?

And more importantly - why?

Do you *really* want what you think you want?

Or do you just believe it will make you happier than you are now? Once you have spent a good amount of time thinking about this, it's time to move to the next step: writing down the things you want in the beginning of your journal.

Action Step: Scribe As If It Is Done

I am love. I am light. I am powerful. I am a creator. I am here to create my experience.

Once you have gotten clear on what you want and why, the next step is for you to write about this as if it is already happening. Write them as if they are already done AND write about why they bring you joy.

This practice is called scribing, and when done correctly, it is one of the most powerful tools of manifestation.

As you write, you are not just describing your dream life - you are feeling it. You are using the writing process to lift your vibration, to step into the energy of this version of you, the one that already exists in the quantum field, waiting for you to claim her.

This is not about wishful thinking. It is about aligning your frequency with the life you desire.

And here's what you must understand…

What you feel fuels your manifestations. Every word you write carries an energetic charge - so if you're writing from a place of doubt, lack, or frustration, you are reinforcing that energy instead of shifting it.

Before you begin, pause. Tune in. How are you feeling?

If you feel light, excited, expansive - good. You are aligned.

If you feel heavy, doubtful, frustrated - pause. Shift your state first.

From now on, your focus is on your vibration. Nothing matters more than how you feel. Your energy is creating your reality.

As you write, let your words move you. Let them pull you into the feeling of already having what you desire. This is the key to making it real.

Here's an example of how this might look:

I am so happy and grateful now that financial abundance flows to me through a variety of different channels. I love that I have broken free from the limitations of my mind and stepped into the truest version of who I came here to be. I see now that limitation was just a story, a belief I was programmed to buy into. I love money flowing to me. I don't need to store it up or cling to it, because I recognise that it is always flowing. I love that I now have the most beautiful relationship with money, that I see her as a consciousness, and that we love to spend time together. I see it was simply my fear that was blocking her flow, and now we work together so that I can fully experience life. The beautiful consciousness of wealth opens so many doors for me and enables me to explore everything I came here to discover. I love not living in fear. I love the freedom I feel in this new relationship. I love the surprises of how abundance finds her way to me. Gosh, this freedom feels good. Gosh, I love to feel like this. This is the most incredible, expansive feeling I have ever had - there really is no limit.

Can you feel these words? What does it feel like as you read them? Can you feel how high frequency they are? Let's try it with something else..

I am so happy and grateful now that I live in the body of my dreams. I love my body. I love to nourish her with high vibrational foods. I love to feel healthy. Healthy is my natural state. I love feeling light in my body, I love that my body feels good and I love to wear clothes that fit me well. I am so happy and grateful now that I am full of energy, I feel the youngest I have felt in years, it feels amazing - gosh this feels good! I love to feel like this. I am full of health and vitality. I look younger than I have for a very long time, my skin is glowing and I am the weight I have always wanted to be. It was so much easier than I realised, I simply needed to stop being so unkind to my body and myself, I needed to start taking loving action and to realise what a miracle this body I live in truly is. I love to feel like this. I love to be healthy and well. I love to dance and move without any restriction or discomfort - this is how I love to be. This is my natural state.

Just let the words flow from your heart and pour them onto the paper with the entire intention of writing to be from your future self and to shift your vibrational frequency. Let us try another area of your life...

I love to be in love with my partner. I love that we have such a deep, intimate and soul based love. My partner is my soul mate. I love how much we laugh together and that we spend time in deep intimacy and connection. I love that we are a team and I feel so seen, safe, and supported. I feel understood and so loved. I now know that I am worthy of a love like this, a love that feels like a dream. This love is full of so much joy and light. It feels wonderful to wake up with this person every day. There is nothing I need to hide any more - I can allow them to see the whole of me and let the love pour in - I know I am worthy of it. I am so happy and excited now that I am with the love of my life and that we are a better fit than I ever possibly imagined. I love how love feels. (You can use words like this to either rekindle an existing relationship, or find new love if you are single!)

Or if you want to start a business, you would write something like...

I have a thriving business that makes an impact in the lives of others around the world. My work brings me great joy and is deeply aligned with the mission I came to this Earth to fulfil. I love getting up in the morning and being of service to others. I love helping people rise up and become a greater version of themselves and live more greatly in alignment with who they came here to be...

Let yourself *feel* as you write. Let your words expand you.

Because this isn't just journaling.

This is creation.

You can make this practice a beautiful ritual. If you like, you can clear the room with sage first, light a candle, put on some gentle music in the background - make this a process you really enjoy and want to come back to.

Do this for every area of your life that you want to shift. Don't overthink it. You don't need to re-read it or analyse it - just write, feel, and let the energy move. You can return to this practice as many times as needed to elevate your state and align with what you desire.

This is where commitment comes in.

How committed are you to taking action every day to create your new life?

Transformation doesn't happen by chance - it happens through intention, focus, and consistency. Your new life requires your time, your energy, and your willingness to show up for it now, before the external evidence appears.

Your challenge: Commit to this practice daily for at least six weeks.

You don't need to cover every area of your life at once. Instead, focus on one aspect at a time and continue until you feel the shift - until your thoughts naturally resonate at a higher vibration.

Feeling the Shift

I want to spend a little time on feeling the shift because this is such a significant step.

Remember, everything is energy, and everything is vibrational. How you feel matters.

Living in alignment means living in coherence - when your heart and mind are vibrating in a frequency that attracts what you do desire rather than what you don't.

Take a moment. Put your hands on your heart. Read these words first, then close your eyes and move through the practice.

Step 1: The Breathwork Shift

Begin by focusing on your breath. Slow it down.

Breathe into your belly, allowing it to expand fully - like a Buddha belly.

- Inhale for a count of four.

- Exhale for a count of six.

- Repeat for several rounds.

Why does this matter?

Because the way you breathe directly affects your nervous system.

If you are breathing shallowly into your chest, you are triggering your sympathetic nervous system - the red zone. This is your fight-or-flight mode. Your body releases stress hormones, shuts down digestion, weakens immunity, and floods you with adrenaline. It believes you are in danger.

In this state, you feel stressed, anxious, and exhausted - and you are not in a frequency that allows you to manifest what you desire.

Your brain shifts into high-beta waves, meaning you are stuck in doing, reacting, and survival mode. This is not coherence. It is not alignment. And over time, it is the beginning of all disease in the body.

Now, breathe deeply into your belly. When you do, you signal to your body:

"All is well. I am safe."

This shifts you into the parasympathetic nervous system - the green zone. Your body moves into homeostasis. Your brainwaves slow down, shifting from beta into alpha - a more relaxed, receptive state.

Step 2: The Heart Activation

Once you feel your body relaxing, bring your awareness to your heart.

Imagine a beautiful golden orb of light glowing at the centre of your chest.

With each inhale, this light expands.

With each exhale, it grows brighter.

Do this for several breaths until you feel the warmth and presence of this light.

Now, bring your awareness to your desires - the ones you clarified in the first step of this journey. Imagine they have already come true.

Smile. Feel the joy in your heart as if you are already living in that reality.

Step 3: Moving into Gratitude

Keep breathing.

Now, shift your awareness to deep gratitude.

Think of the people, experiences, and moments that bring you joy.

Think of the children in your life, their sweet innocence, their wonder.

Think of a moment when you felt pure peace - maybe walking in nature, feeling the sun on your skin.

Think of the joy of simple things - the smell of fresh coffee, the comfort of your favourite book, the way your pet looks at you with unconditional love.

Let the feeling of gratitude **expand within you.**

Step 4: Aligning with the Universe

This feeling is coherence.

This is the frequency that aligns you with the universe.

This is the space where **manifestation begins.**

When you hold this vibration, **you are no longer pushing, striving, or forcing life to happen.**

You are in the flow.

And from here, life will begin to shift.

Action step: Spend 15 minutes practicing this every day. If you do this on a daily basis - you will begin to notice a significant change in the way you feel and your outer experience will begin to change. In four tiny weeks! You can do that, right? Commit to 15 minutes a day!

Top Tip: The 17-Second Rule

Physics has shown us that like attracts like after just 17 seconds of focused attention on a vibration.

This is why spending time raising your focus to higher frequencies is so powerful. After just 17 seconds, your mind begins to attract another thought of a similar frequency, then another, and another. Before you know it, your mind is flooded with high-vibrational thoughts, shifting your entire state.

Your job? Notice your emotional frequency throughout the day.

Stay aware of what you're focusing on, because your energy is always attracting more of the same.

Action Step: Commit to a New Morning

I am love. I am light. I am powerful. I am a creator. I am here to create my experience.

Every morning, you wake up with a brand-new blank canvas. A fresh start. Pure, untapped potential.

The only thing that makes today feel like yesterday is your thinking.

Your patterns. Your habits. Your default way of waking up and carrying on as if nothing has changed.

But something is changing. You are changing.

And if you truly want a different life, you have to start by doing things differently.

This is where the real question comes in:

How much do you want things to change?

How much do you really want to experience your dream life? How much are you willing to shift, to break the old patterns, to take ownership of your energy?

Your morning is sacred. It is the only part of the day that hasn't yet been shaped by your old stories, your limiting beliefs, or the noise of the world.

And it is time for you to claim it.

I am going to ask you to give yourself time - real time - to start your day in a completely different way.

This is not just about a "better morning routine."

This is about setting the energy of your entire life in motion. There is no room for your old programming; there is no room for negative thinking.

Are you willing to meet your future self here?

Because if you are, everything starts to shift.

In this step, you are going to commit to getting up earlier and becoming aware of how you think from the moment you open your eyes. If I had to name one action step as the most important, this might be it.

This is a key component of your transformation.

You must dedicate a portion of your morning to shifting your frequency.

How much time you can give yourself will depend on your life, your responsibilities, and your current habits. Maybe you have young children, maybe you like to sleep in, or maybe your old story is, *"I'm just not a morning person."*

But here's the truth: if you really want to change your life, you will find a way. No matter what challenges you face, no matter how many excuses your mind tries to give you.

You will either make it happen or you won't.

I have coached so many women through the *"I struggle to get out of bed in the morning"* story. And the truth is - you have to decide to stop repeating that narrative and fight for yourself.

If you are hitting snooze, lying in bed thinking about how much you don't want to face the day, or scrolling your phone before you've even gotten up - how can you expect your life to be different?

Nothing will change unless you change it.

It's time to shake things up.

When I left my corporate job to become a yoga teacher, I was a single mother. I had to get up an hour earlier every day just to practice yoga before my son woke up, so that I could be present with him and get him ready for school.

At the time, I didn't realise that this simple shift would become one of the biggest reasons my life transformed so radically.

But it did.

Because I radically changed my morning routine - and therefore, my vibration.

I went from waking up late, dreading the day, and scrolling my phone first thing… to spending my mornings taking care of my body, connecting to my inner wisdom, and aligning with the frequency of love.

And that was the key to my transformation.

Now, we are going to change your morning.

Decide what time you are going to wake up - and commit to it. No more negotiating, no more hitting snooze. Make the decision, and just do it.

Think about the person you are becoming. The version of you who is already living the life you desire - how do they start their day?

What time do they wake up and with what attitude? Gratitude and joy or heaviness and frustration? What do they do in the morning to set themselves up for success? What choices do they make to align their energy before they step into the world?

If you want to embody the greatest version of yourself, start living as they would now.

One simple but powerful change: keep your phone out of your bedroom.

I strongly encourage you not to use your phone as an alarm or keep it by your bed. Your nervous system is not designed to wake up and immediately absorb notifications, messages, or emails.

If you want to create new habits, the best thing you can do is start by doing things differently - right from the moment you wake up.

Get an old-school alarm clock and set it to the time you are now committed to.

Now, let's talk about transformation…

The beginning of any change will come with resistance.

The old version of you will fight to keep things the same - even if that version is struggling.

This is where you have to get out of your own way.

Your ego thrives on keeping you comfortable, even when that comfort is holding you back. It will try to convince you to stay in bed, to wait for motivation, to start *tomorrow* instead.

But if you really want change, you have to fight for it.

Think about building strength at the gym. It's uncomfortable at first. You push through resistance, your muscles ache, and at times, it feels easier to quit.

Yet over time, you get stronger.

And it's not just your body that strengthens - it's your mind, your discipline, your ability to keep going when it feels hard.

This is the same.

There will be discomfort. There will be moments when you don't feel like it.

But you can handle it.

You are stronger than your resistance.

And as you push through, you will find a power inside you that has been there all along.

So decide what you are going to do, and do it.

No stories. No *"I'll try."* No *"this is too hard."*

Just do it (like that well known trainer brand!) Once you have committed to the time, we now need to talk about how you are going to spend it.

Action Step: Decide What to Do with Your Reclaimed Space in the Morning

I am love. I am light. I am powerful. I am a creator. I am here to create my experience. Your morning is the most powerful opportunity you have to shift your energy.

It sets the tone for everything that follows. This is the moment to intentionally elevate your frequency - to align yourself with the energy you want to carry through your day.

But before we dive into *how*, let's get clear on *why*. What is success, really?

It's not more stuff. It's not more money. It's not the perfect body or the ideal career.

It's peace.

Because beneath every desire, what you're truly seeking is freedom from the entrapment of the mind. When you master your inner world - when you align to peace - you unlock a level of freedom that no external achievement can ever give you.

And this is why mastering your mind matters so much.

The practices that shift your brain waves from Beta (the busy, action - driven state) into Alpha, Gamma, or even Theta are what will raise your vibration and align you to the frequency of the divine.

But what does that really mean?

Your brain operates at different frequencies throughout the day - each one influencing your thoughts, emotions, and ability to connect with higher states of awareness.

- Beta is where most people live - fast-paced, analytical, often stressed. It's the state of *doing*, constantly reacting to the world, problem - solving, and thinking ahead. While necessary for daily tasks, being stuck in Beta keeps you disconnected from your deeper wisdom.

- Alpha is the bridge between the conscious and subconscious mind. It's the state of relaxed awareness, where intuition strengthens, creativity flows, and ideas come effortlessly. This is why meditation, deep breathing, or even a quiet walk can shift you into Alpha and instantly change your energy.

- Theta is even deeper. It's the frequency of dreaming, deep meditation, and profound inner healing. In Theta, your subconscious is wide open, making it the most powerful state for rewiring beliefs, accessing intuition, and connecting to the divine.

- Gamma is the highest vibration state. It's where elevated consciousness, peak intuition, and profound moments of insight occur. Mystical experiences, deep gratitude, and feelings of oneness with the universe are all linked to Gamma waves.

So when we talk about raising your vibration, we're really talking about training your mind to shift out of Beta and into these higher states more often.

And the beautiful part? You don't have to *force* it.

Simple practices like meditation, visualisation, breathwork, gratitude, stillness, and even intentional movement can gently bring your brain waves into alignment with your higher self.

This is why a morning practice matters so much. It's not about just "doing" something spiritual - it's about shifting your state, setting your energy, and moving into your day from a place of alignment rather than reaction.

Because the more time you spend in these higher frequencies, the more naturally you begin to create from peace, love, and limitless possibility.

Letting Go to Let it Flow

I am love. I am light. I am powerful. I am a creator. I am here to create my experience.

If you want to create the life of your dreams, you must be willing to let go of the illusion that "more" will make you worthy.

The mindset of "I need more to be enough" is keeping you in a state of lack - and that lack is blocking your manifestations.

So what do you do with this time in the morning?

You break the pattern of your old self.

You break the pattern of attachment and limitation.

You come home to peace and you shift your energy to a higher frequency through the nourishment of your three bodies:

- **Your Spirit Body**

- **Your Soul Body**

- **Your Physical Body**

These three energy centres need your care. And when you nourish all three, your vibration will raise and your manifestations will begin to flow.

Let's say you have committed one hour in the morning to change your life.

This hour is yours.

And what you do with it will determine everything.

I am going to give you a list of different practices so that you can choose what resonates with you. The key is to break your hour down into sections that nourish each of your three bodies - Spirit, Soul, and Physical.

Action Step: Nourishing Your Spirit Body

I am love. I am light. I am powerful. I am a creator. I am here to create my experience.

Your Spirit needs nourishment through prayer and gratitude. I love to combine these two practices, and over time, you will find the way that feels most natural to you.

Your Spirit is the truth of who you are.

And part of the reason the world is in so much turmoil - the only reason - is because people have forgotten who they really are.

If you truly knew yourself as Spirit first, you would not feel lack. You would not feel fear. You would know what you are capable of.

But we have become so entangled in the physical world that we have lost touch with our infinite nature.

Nourishing your Spirit is about coming home to your truth.

To the expansiveness of who you are.

To the part of you that is eternal, limitless, and wise beyond measure.

This is why this practice matters - because when you connect to your highest self, you rise above the illusions of limitation.

There is a part of you - the quiet observer - who has been waiting.

Waiting for you to pause. Waiting for you to sit in stillness. Waiting for you to wake up and remember.

Come home.

And listen. So nourish her, care for her and love her. She is you. Here is my example of prayer that you might like to use or play with and adapt so that it works for you.

Dear Mother, Father, God…
Thank you.
Thank you for this life. For the sacred opportunity of this physical experience. For the breath that moves through me, the heart that beats within me, the light that guides me home to myself.

Thank you for the love I have been given - the love I share, the love I receive, the love that flows endlessly through all things. Thank you for the relationships in my life, each one a mirror, each one a teacher, each one guiding me deeper into the remembrance of who I truly am.

Thank you for the moments of stillness, where I hear you whisper in the quiet.

Thank you for the challenges, the trials, the times when I have fallen to my knees - because even in those moments, you were there. Because even in my struggle, I was never alone.

Thank you for the lessons, the growth, the unfolding of this divine path. Thank you for the expansion that comes with every breath, with every step, with every sunrise that greets me anew.

Thank you for the unseen forces of love that surround me. For the angels who walk beside me, for the guidance that is always available when I soften, when I listen, when I trust.

Thank you for the beauty of this world. For the sky that stretches endlessly above me, for the earth that cradles me beneath my feet. For the rivers, the oceans, the trees that breathe with me, that remind me I am part of something vast, something eternal, something infinitely woven in love.

But above all, thank you for who I am.

Help me remember.

Help me remember that I am not separate from you, that I am made in your image, that the power of creation flows through me.

Help me remember that it is I who is the creator - that my thoughts, my energy, and my beliefs shape the world I experience.

Help me remember that nothing is outside of me - that I am not at the mercy of circumstance, but that I hold the power to create the reality of my dreams.

Help me remember my strength, my divinity, my infinite potential.

Help me release all that keeps me small - all fear, all doubt, all illusion that tells me I am anything less than whole, anything less than capable, anything less than love itself.

I surrender to you. I surrender my fears, my doubts, my resistance. I release all that is heavy, all that is untrue, all that keeps me from resting in the deep peace of your presence.

Let me be a vessel of your light. Let me walk in love. Let me see the divinity in all things, in all people, in myself.

May I live in remembrance. May I move in grace. May I be a reflection of the love that created me.

I am here. I am listening. I am ready.

And for all of this, for all that I see and all that I do not yet understand, for all that has been, and all that is still to come…

Thank you.

Thank you.

Thank you.

Prayer is not just saying words - it is using words to shift your frequency and it is entirely possible for us to transform ourselves and our world through the use of prayer. Prayer is not begging God for something to happen - it is using words to change yourself.

Every word carries energy. Every word creates.

All spells are spoken. All magick is spoken. Every manifestation begins as a vibration.

When you pray, when you speak, when you declare - your words are casting energetic ripples into the universe. But if those words are empty, if they are spoken without feeling, without heart, without presence, they hold no power.

To truly create, you must feel the words you speak. You must know them to be true.

You must let them move through your body, your heart, your being - because words spoken with conviction, with love, with deep certainty - those are the words that shape reality.

Everything is vibrational.

Every word you utter, every thought you hold, every belief you reinforce creates a frequency that life responds to.

So speak with intention.

Use your words wisely.

Use them with love.

Use them with the respect they deserve.

Because what you speak, you summon.

With this in mind, I invite you to begin your mornings by using scripting and prayer to elevate your vibration.

The first thing you do is get out of bed and scribe - write from the perspective of your future self, the version of you who already exists in the highest frequency. Let this method pull you into alignment. Let it shift your energy so that you are not just thinking about the life you desire - you are feeling it.

Once you have used scripting to lift your state, you can then move into prayer - a practice to nourish your Soul, anchor gratitude, and connect to the divine.

In total, this will take no more than 15 minutes - yet these 15 minutes have the power to change everything.

And now, with 45 minutes left in play, it's time to nourish your Soul.

Action Step: Nourishing Your Soul Body

I am love. I am light. I am powerful. I am a creator. I am here to create my experience. Your Soul craves stillness, creativity, and solitude.

It longs for beauty, silence, and spaciousness.

It deserves to be nourished, to be listened to, to be felt.

You may not like what I'm about to say, but meditation is one of the most important keys to your transformation.

Why?

Because you need to escape the noise of your mind and connect with the truth of who you are.

Most people try to drown out that noise with busyness, distractions, and avoidance. They run from silence because sitting with themselves feels uncomfortable.

They try to escape their own thoughts through eating, drinking, sex, shopping, scrolling, gossiping, work, drugs - anything to avoid the discomfort.

And trust me - I tried it all. I tried really hard.

But it never works.

It only pulls you deeper into the very energy you're trying to escape. It lowers your frequency. It keeps you stuck in the loop of avoidance and disconnection. **All healing takes place through stillness**.

The only way to truly shift and transform is by going within - not doing more without.

There is no way around it.

If you want to create a new life for yourself, you must learn how to be still. You must learn how to face what you've been running from. You must learn how to meet yourself in silence - because in that silence, you will finally hear the truth.

And that truth?

It will set you free.

So, you guessed it - the next step is meditation.

You've used scribing and prayer to elevate your vibration. Now, it's time to focus on that feeling and move into stillness.

I suggest starting with 20 minutes. We talked earlier about getting into heart coherence. This is where you can use this practice. Use your meditation time to get into heart coherence and practice for 20 minutes every day. Here is where I really want you to commit to this.

In fact, I'll make you a deal. If you commit to meditating every day for six weeks and you don't feel different, you can personally write to me, and I'll give you all your money back for this book. I'm that confident.

Just yesterday, a client said to me, "I am so annoyed - you were right! I have been meditating every day for six weeks, and I feel completely different. I'm receiving insight and wisdom I could never access before. I hate that you were right!"

That's what happens when you give this practice a real chance.

Now, if 20 minutes feels impossible for you right now, start with what you can - but start. Any amount of stillness is better than none. We build from where we are.

Once you've chosen your time, set a timer with a gentle alarm and commit.

Your mind will try to distract you. Let it.

Your thoughts will wander. Let them.

Your job is not to have a "perfect" meditation - your job is to sit, stay, and train yourself in stillness.

The mastery of your mind is key.

If you don't learn how to direct your thoughts, they will continue to direct you.

And if you're thinking, *"But I'm not good at meditating,"* I hear you. I've heard it a thousand times before.

And I'll tell you what I tell every client:

You are good at meditating.

You just need to practice.

Because how do we get good at anything?

We show up.

We keep going.

We practice.

And that is exactly what you are going to do.

Here are some top meditation tips…

Meditation Tip One

Pop on some gentle, soothing music without words. You can search for high frequency meditation music on Spotify or any of the music channels and you will find plenty of options there. Classical music is also very good, like Beethoven or Bach - any music you find soothing.

Meditation Tip Two

Sit in a chair with your feet on the ground (uncross your legs and place both feet on the earth) so that energy can run through your body evenly. You can place your hands on your lap with your palms facing up so that you are in the position to receive.

Meditation Tip Three

Don't try to quieten your mind. The job of your mind is to chatter. If you attempt to fight with it, it will fight back. This is the number one way many people go wrong and believe they cannot meditate. The trick instead is to draw your attention away from the mind and come into the body (practice the heart coherence we covered earlier). Bring your attention to your heart and to your breath. Follow your breath in and your breath out.

Meditation Tip Four

Gently press your tongue to the roof of your mouth. This helps quieten your mind, and direct your energy and focus.

Meditation Tip Five

Don't worry if your mind wanders, simply bring it back as soon as you notice and come back to your breath and your heart. Don't try and perfect this, simply be with it.

Meditation is a practice.

Apply these steps in your mediation practice every day and you will find that your meditation improves greatly very quickly and that you even enjoy it! Meditation is important for so many reasons - it will allow you to develop your intuition, it will enable you to overcome your ego and master your mind, it will shift your resonance and raise your vibration, it will improve the quality of your thinking so that you are manifesting what you do want, rather than what you don't. So this is an important step!

Action Step: Nourishing Your Physical Body

I am love. I am light. I am powerful. I am a creator. I am here to create my experience.

If you've given yourself an hour in the morning, you've already spent 35 minutes scribing, envisioning, praying, expressing gratitude, and meditating. You are now starting your day from a much more powerful place.

The final step is nourishing your physical body. Your body is not who you are - it is the temple in which you reside. You cannot have a physical experience without it, and how your body feels directly impacts your vibration. Take care of it well, but remember, you are not your body.

Everything you eat carries vibration, and certain foods will naturally make you feel better, clearer, and more energised than others. Choose natural, whole foods - home-cooked meals, fresh fruits and vegetables, foods filled with life force energy. The more colours on your plate, the higher vibrational your meal. Starting your day with a green juice or a nourishing smoothie is an excellent way to flood your body with nutrients.

You are 70% water, and water purifies and cleanses your system. Make sure you are drinking at least 2 litres of water daily - ideally more. Hydration isn't just about health; it's about clarity, flow, and vibrational alignment.

You will want to reduce caffeine, which triggers the red zone and takes you out of flow; as well as sugar and processed foods, as they lower vibration and impact your energy.

Take a moment to reflect: what small changes can you make to nourish yourself better? How can you add more vibrant, nutrient-dense foods into your daily routine? Because while you may not have thought that what you eat impacts your manifestation ability, it absolutely does. If you feel heavy, sluggish, or inflamed, this affects your entire energy field, making it harder to be in flow.

Movement is key to energy flow. Your body is meant to move. Movement shifts stagnant energy, raises your vibration, and grounds you into the present moment. Choose what feels good for you - yoga, qigong, running, weight training, dancing, or walking. It doesn't need to be long - just 20 minutes of daily movement can change how you feel. If you don't know where to start, YouTube has endless free classes.

So with your remaining 25 minutes, focus on hydration, movement, and nourishing your body with high-vibrational foods. Because when you feed your body well, hydrate deeply, and move daily, you don't just feel good - you align with the frequency of your highest self.

So now you have gotten clear and committed, it is time to move to the R in CREATE.

CHAPTER 8

RAISE YOUR FREQUENCY

I am love. I am light. I am powerful.
I am a creator. I am here to create
my experience.

All of the above commitments will already raise your frequency. If you shift your morning in the way I have outlined and you commit to a daily practice of heart coherence and mediation - my goodness, you have already done incredible things. Remember, your frequency is the most important thing to think about moving forward. Here are some things to work on to help you raise your frequency even further.

1. The Power of Gratitude

Gratitude is one of the most powerful forces in the universe. It has the ability to shift your entire life, aligning you with the flow of powerful manifestation. There are countless stories of people healing their bodies, making extraordinary financial shifts,

transforming relationships, and turning their lives around - simply by practicing gratitude.

It is said: If you are not grateful, you will never have enough.

Remember, what you focus on expands. Start getting grateful for what you do have, and stop placing your attention on what you don't.

Finances are a perfect example of this. Most people look at their bank account and think, *I don't have enough.* Stop doing that immediately. Every time you affirm lack, you attract more of it into your life. Instead, shift your perspective. Be grateful for every bit of money that has ever come into your life - the education you've received, the holidays you've taken, the home you live in, the comforts you enjoy, the food on your table, the gifts you've been given. If you start focusing on where wealth already exists in your life, you will immediately shift your vibration, allowing even more abundance to flow to you.

You live in an abundant and unlimited universe. The only limitation is the way you think. What you think, you create.

The same is true for your health. How often do you criticise your body? How many times have you looked in the mirror and rejected what you see? Do you wake up in the morning grateful for another day, or do you immediately focus on what feels wrong? Do you go to bed at night thanking your body for carrying you through the day, or do you dwell on how tired you are?

You are creating your reality. The more gratitude you express for the things you want to improve, the more they will shift in your favour. Your frequency determines what flows to you - gratitude raises that frequency like nothing else.

Action Step: Daily Gratitude Practice

Every day, write down ten things you are deeply grateful for - and feel the feeling of gratitude in your body. It can be the same ten things every day; they don't have to be different. What matters is the emotion behind the practice.

Your gratitude list can include **the smallest things** - a warm cup of tea, a flower blooming, the sound of laughter. **They all matter.** The more you appreciate the small things, the more you will receive the big things.

2. The Power of Belief

Your beliefs shape everything. They are the invisible architects of your reality, the lens through which you see the world, and the energy you unconsciously project into every situation.

Here's the truth most people miss - your beliefs are not facts. They are just stories you have told yourself (or been told) over and over again until they became so deeply ingrained that they feel like absolute truth. But a belief is nothing more than a thought repeated enough times that your mind accepts it as reality.

If your beliefs are empowering, they will create a life of possibility and expansion. But if your beliefs are rooted in lack, fear, or unworthiness, they will keep you stuck in loops of struggle and limitation - not because the world is against you, but because you are unknowingly affirming the very circumstances you wish to change. This is why shifting your beliefs is one of the most powerful things you can do.

If you want to understand why your life looks the way it does, take a moment to reflect on the core beliefs you hold about yourself and the world. Ask yourself: **What do I believe about money?** Is it hard to earn? Does it require struggle? **What do I believe about love?** Am I worthy of deep love, or do I fear being abandoned? **What do I believe about success?** Do I think I'm capable of achieving my dreams, or do I always feel like I'm falling short? **What do I believe about myself?** Do I trust my power, or do I question my worth?

Your outer world is reflecting these inner beliefs back to you every single day. If you don't like what you see in your reality, it's time to rewrite the story. Changing a belief doesn't happen instantly - it happens through awareness, repetition, and embodiment. Here's how:

1. Identify the belief - What is the thought that keeps looping in your mind? Write it down.

2. Question its truth - Is this belief absolutely true? Has it been proven in every circumstance?

3. Find counter-evidence - Look for examples (even small ones) where the opposite was true. If you believe money is hard to make, think of a time when it flowed to you effortlessly.

4. Rewrite it - Turn the old belief into an empowering new truth. Instead of *"I'm not good enough,"* shift it to *"I am more than enough, just as I am."*

5. Reinforce it daily - Speak it, affirm it, and most importantly - act in alignment with it.

A belief shifts when you stop waiting for external proof and start embodying it now.

Action Step: The Belief Rewiring Practice

Every day, write down one limiting belief that is holding you back. Then, challenge it. Ask: Is this actually true? Write down three reasons why it's not true - real-life examples that prove otherwise.

Now, rewrite it into an empowering new belief and say it out loud to yourself. Repeat this daily until the new belief feels as natural and familiar as the old one once did. Because when you change your beliefs, you change your life.

3. The Power of Thought

Your mind is the starting point for everything you create. Every outcome in your life - your success, relationships, health, and abundance - is a reflection of the thoughts you consistently think.

Most people don't realise that their thinking is on autopilot - repeating the same stories, judgements, and assumptions day after day, unknowingly shaping their reality with the same old patterns. But your thoughts are not just passive ideas floating through your head. They are energy. They hold weight. They create.

If your thoughts are rooted in fear, doubt, or negativity, they will shape a reality that reflects those very emotions. If your thoughts are rooted in possibility, gratitude, and expansion, you will attract experiences that match that vibration. This is not wishful thinking; this is energetic law.

If you want to change your life, you must first change your thoughts.

If you want to understand why your life looks the way it does, take a moment to reflect on your dominant thought patterns. Ask yourself: What are the first thoughts I have in the morning? Do I wake up dreading the day, or do I wake up with gratitude and excitement? What do I tell myself when things don't go as planned? Do I spiral into frustration, or do I trust that things are working out for me? How do I think about myself when I look in the mirror? With kindness, or with criticism?

Your mind is constantly narrating your life - shaping your experience moment by moment. If you want to shift your reality, you have to take control of the narrative.

How to Shift Your Thinking

Your thoughts are like seeds. What you plant, you grow. What you repeat, you reinforce. The key is to become intentional about what you are planting in your mind. Here's how:

1. Become aware of your thoughts - Notice the mental loops that play in your mind throughout the day. Pay attention to your inner dialogue.

2. Interrupt negative thought patterns - The moment you catch yourself thinking a limiting or negative thought, pause. Ask yourself: Would I choose to believe this if I knew it was creating my reality?

3. Reframe and redirect - Instead of *"Nothing ever works out for me,"* shift it to *"Things are always working in my favour."* Instead of *"I'm so behind,"* shift it to *"I'm exactly where I'm meant to be."*

4. Use your thoughts to elevate your energy - The fastest way to shift your frequency is to shift your thinking. Choose thoughts that expand you, energise you, and make you feel good in the moment.

5. Make it a habit - Repetition is key. Your thoughts create neural pathways in your brain - if you want new pathways, you must practice new thinking daily.

Your mind is not your master; it is your tool. When you learn to use it intentionally, everything changes.

Action Step: The Thought Awareness Practice

Every day, become conscious of the thoughts you are thinking. Take five minutes to write down the dominant thoughts that ran through your mind that day. Notice patterns - where are your thoughts limiting you? Where are they empowering you? Choose one thought that does not serve you, and rewrite it into a new, powerful thought. Then, repeat that new thought to yourself throughout the day. The more you reinforce it, the faster your mind will adopt it as truth.

Because when you change your thinking, you change your frequency. And when you change your frequency, you change everything.

4. The Power of Where You Place Your Attention

Your time, your energy, and your attention are the currencies of your life. How you spend them determines what you create, how you feel, and what flows into your reality.

Most people don't realise that every moment of their day, they are either raising or lowering their frequency based on what they consume, engage with, and give energy to. Your environment - what you listen to, what you watch, what you talk about - is shaping your vibration just as much as your thoughts.

If you are constantly absorbing negativity, drama, or low - vibrational content, it doesn't just pass through you - it embeds into your energy field. You may not even notice it at first, but over time, it affects your mood, your mindset, and your ability to manifest.

Ask yourself:

- What am I feeding my mind daily? Am I consuming content that inspires, uplifts, and expands me, or am I mindlessly scrolling through negativity?

- Who do I surround myself with? Do the conversations I engage in make me feel energised and aligned, or do they drain me?

- How much of my time is spent in distraction? Do I start my mornings with presence, or do I immediately pick up my phone and get lost in noise?

If you want to raise your frequency, you must become deliberate about what you give your attention to.

How to Protect Your Energy and Elevate Your Frequency

1. Cut out gossip and drama - Gossip may seem harmless, but it's one of the fastest ways to lower your vibration. The energy you put out is the energy you attract - if you engage in tearing others down, you pull yourself down with it.

2. Stop mindless scrolling - Social media can be a powerful tool, but it can also be an energetic drain. Pay attention to how you feel after scrolling. If it leaves you feeling depleted, anxious, or in comparison mode, it's time to set boundaries.

3. Limit exposure to negative news - Staying informed is important, but drowning in the world's chaos does not serve you or the collective. Your energy is needed in solution, not fear. Choose to be aware without being consumed.

4. Surround yourself with high - vibrational conversations - Spend time with people who uplift and expand you. Have conversations that inspire, that challenge you to grow, that remind you of what's possible.

5. Feed your mind with what expands you - Instead of scrolling, read books that elevate your thinking. Instead of watching the news first thing in the morning, listen to something that fuels your

soul. Instead of gossip, speak words of kindness, truth, and empowerment.

Your time, your energy, and your attention are sacred. Where you place them is where your life will expand.

Action Step: The Energy Audit

For the next 24 hours, pay attention to how you are spending your time. Notice the conversations you engage in, the content you consume, and the activities that fill your day. Write down anything that feels like an energy drain - whether it's social media, complaining, gossip, or mindless distraction. Then, make a conscious decision to replace one low-energy habit with something that elevates you instead.

Your energy is your responsibility. Protect it. Elevate it. Use it to create the life you truly desire.

5. The Power of Healing

Healing and energy work aren't just about feeling better in the moment - they are about removing the deeper layers of resistance and misalignment that have been preventing you from fully stepping into your power.

These are a few powerful ways to raise your frequency.

Life Activation

A Life Activation is a profound energetic awakening that infuses your entire system with pure Light. This ancient modality activates your DNA energetically, awakening dormant codes of potential that allow you to step into more of who you truly are. It clears out deep, unseen blockages that may be keeping you stuck in old patterns, elevating your vibration and bringing you into greater alignment with your divine purpose. After a Life Activation, many people experience increased clarity and intuition, more energy and motivation, a sense of purpose and direction, the release of old emotional patterns, and a greater connection to their higher self. It is a profound first step for anyone looking to truly shift their life at the core level.

Full Spirit Activation

Where Life Activation awakens your DNA, Full Spirit Activation takes things even deeper by activating your soul connection to the physical body. This healing allows more of your divine essence to fully integrate, empowering you to live life with more presence, joy, and awareness. It enhances your ability to navigate life with greater clarity, make aligned decisions, and step fully into your power. This is for those who feel they are ready to embody their full spiritual nature in physical form - to not just awaken to their light but to fully live as that light in the world.

Ensofic Reiki

Ensofic Reiki is the purest form of Reiki energy, drawing directly from the Ensofic Ray, which is the highest vibrational energy available to us. Unlike traditional Reiki, which works on the emotional and energetic layers, Ensofic Reiki works at the deepest level of alignment, clearing distortions in the mind and bringing you back to your original divine blueprint. Some of the benefits include profound physical and emotional healing, clearing of mental stress and confusion, bringing deep inner peace and alignment, and restoring the body's natural ability to heal. If you've ever felt off-balance, disconnected, or weighed down by stress and emotions, Ensofic Reiki has the power to realign you at the source.

Initiation Into Higher Consciousness

Initiation is the process of stepping into a higher level of empowerment, awareness, and spiritual connection. In the lineage of King Salomon, initiation is a sacred rite of passage that allows you to anchor more Light into your being and walk through life with greater clarity, strength, and purpose. Through initiation, you receive energetic keys that unlock deeper levels of wisdom, protection, and manifestation ability. This is an accelerator for spiritual growth and transformation, setting you on a path of greater self-mastery.

How This Transforms Your Life

When you combine these ancient tools with the daily practices we've discussed, you elevate your entire energetic system. You move from just *thinking about change* to embodying it at the deepest level.

This is why energy work is so powerful - it works at the root level. It activates what is already within you, allowing you to experience the highest version of yourself in this lifetime.

Action Step: Explore Healing & Energy Work

Take a moment to reflect on where you feel stuck or misaligned in your life. Do you feel blocked in your purpose? Are you struggling with old emotional wounds? Are you ready to step into more of who you truly are? Consider which healing modality calls to you. If you feel drawn to Life Activation, Full Spirit Activation, Ensofic Reiki, or Initiation, trust that your soul is guiding you toward the next step in your expansion. Because when you heal your energy, everything shifts.

And now we move to E ...

CHAPTER 9

EMBODY THE ENERGY

I am love. I am light. I am powerful.
I am a creator. I am here to create
my experience.

Now that you've learned how to raise your frequency, the next step is to live from that elevated state. Remember: you don't manifest what you want - you manifest what you are.

Many people do the inner work, feel the shift, raise their vibration - but then they go back to living the same way, making the same choices, and reacting from their old patterns.

If you want to create something new in your life, you must become the person who already has it.

This is the **art of being rather than doing** - the essence of the Divine Feminine. The masculine energy is all about action, force, and structure. The feminine energy is about receptivity, presence, intuition, trust, and allowing life to flow through you.

To embody the energy of what you desire, you must **soften into the knowing that it is already yours**.

You do not need to chase it. You do not need to force it. You simply need to become the energetic match for it, and let it come to you.

What Embodying the Energy Looks Like

1. Feel it first. Ask yourself, *How does the version of me who already has what I desire feel on a daily basis?* If she feels free, successful, radiant, at peace - then it's time to start cultivating those feelings now, before anything in your external world changes.

2. Move through life as if it's already done. When you wake up in the morning, set the intention: *I am already the person who has the life I desire. How would I show up today?* Embody that energy in your posture, your tone, your presence, and your thoughts.

3. Shift how you speak. Words hold power. If you constantly say, *I'm trying, I hope, maybe one day,* you are affirming that your desires are out of reach. Instead, say, *I am becoming, I trust, I know it's unfolding.* Your language should reflect your certainty.

4. Lean into trust and receptivity. The Divine Feminine does not rush or push - she magnetises. She knows she is worthy of receiving. She flows, she allows, she listens to her inner knowing. Manifestation is not about striving - it is about aligning, holding, and receiving.

5. Stop looking for proof - be the proof. Many people look around and think, *I'll believe it when I see it.* But manifestation works the other way around. You must believe it first, embody it fully, and then watch as reality reshapes itself around you.

The moment you start living from the energy of your desired reality, you step into a powerful new frequency where opportunities, people, and experiences naturally align with you. This is how manifestation moves from theoretical to inevitable.

Action Step: Embody Your Future Self Now

For the next seven days, practice living as the version of you who already has what you desire.

Each morning, ask yourself: *How does my future self feel? How does she move through the world? How does she hold her energy? What does she no longer entertain in her energy field?*

At the end of the day, reflect on how you **showed up differently.** Did you think differently? Speak differently? Feel more at peace? Did you notice yourself surrendering more, trusting more, and allowing more?

The more you **consciously embody this energy**, the faster your external world will shift to match it.

Because when you **become her now, reality has no choice but to catch up.**

The next step is A...

CHAPTER 10

ACT IN ALIGNMENT

I am love. I am light. I am powerful.
I am a creator. I am here to create
my experience.

Now that you've raised your frequency and embodied the energy of your future self, it's time to take the next step: aligned action. This is where **manifestation meets momentum.**

Alignment is everything. **Energy flows from the non-physical into the physical**, and when you are out of alignment, that flow becomes blocked. This is what causes struggle, resistance, and pain. It's why so many people numb themselves - because they are living out of alignment with who they truly are.

Alignment means to be in flow. To live as Spirit in the physical world. To remember who you are and to come home to your truth. You were born to live in abundant flow, because in truth, there is no lack. When you feel stuck, disconnected, or limited, it's simply because you are moving out of alignment with your divine essence.

Your internal guidance system is always showing you where you are. When you don't feel good - whether it's doubt, fear, frustration, or lack - you are out of alignment. Your thinking is misaligned with the truth of who you are. When you feel expansive, joyful, and trusting, you are in alignment. You are in flow.

You can always tell where you are. The measure is how you feel.

This is why taking action is essential. When you act in alignment, you move with the current of life instead of against it. But this does not mean taking action from a place of fear, stress, or force. It means taking action from trust, joy, and embodied energy.

What Acting in Alignment Looks Like

1. Step out of your comfort zone. Growth does not happen in the familiar. The version of you who already has what you desire has already moved through fear and doubt. You must do the same. Lean into discomfort. Expand your edges. Take the leap.

2. Make decisions from your future self. Before making any choice, ask: *What would the version of me who already has my dream life do?* Then - do that. Live from her energy, her certainty, and her wisdom.

3. Let go of the need to control. Aligned action is not about forcing things to happen - it's about **trusting the process** and taking inspired action without attachment to the outcome. Move for-

ward with confidence, but surrender the *how* and *when.*

4. Keep going. This is the biggest secret of all: *The people who succeed are simply the ones who didn't quit.* Keep taking steps, even when doubt creeps in. Not from a place of stress, fear, or forcing - but from a place of **trust, joy, and embodied energy.**

5. Take action before you feel "ready." If you wait for the perfect moment, the perfect conditions, the perfect plan - you will stay exactly where you are. **Action creates clarity.** You don't need to know every step, you just need to take the next one.

When you combine high-frequency energy with consistent, aligned action, manifestation becomes inevitable.

Action Step: Move Beyond Your Comfort Zone

For the next seven days, commit to one bold action each day that stretches you beyond your comfort zone. It doesn't have to be massive - just something that moves you forward. Ask yourself daily: *What action would my future self take today? Where am I holding back out of fear? What small step can I take that aligns with my highest vision?*

At the end of the week, reflect: How did taking action shift my energy? What opportunities or synchronicities arose? What felt uncomfortable, and how did I move through it?

Because when you show up for your dreams, consistently and courageously, the universe shows up for you. **And the next step is T.**

CHAPTER 11

TRUST IN THE PROCESS

I am love. I am light. I am powerful.
I am a creator. I am here to create
my experience.

The next step in CREATE is one that so many people struggle with: trusting in the process. You've raised your frequency, embodied the energy, and taken aligned action - but now you must let go and trust that what you desire is already on its way to you.

This is where most people block their manifestations. They do the work, but then they start doubting. They look around and don't see immediate results, so they question whether it's working. They get impatient, frustrated, and start trying to force things into place.

But trust is the key that keeps everything in flow.

If you plant a seed, you don't dig it up every day to check if it's growing. You trust that as long as it has water, sunlight, and the right conditions, it will sprout in divine timing. Your manifestations are the same. If you constantly doubt, worry, and micromanage the process, you block the very thing you are calling in.

Trust does not mean sitting back and doing nothing - it means knowing that everything is unfolding exactly as it should, even when you can't yet see the results.

What Trusting the Process Looks Like

1. Release attachment to the timeline. Your desires are already on their way, but they may not arrive in the exact way or timing you expect. The universe works in perfect order, and your job is to trust that things are happening for you, not against you.

2. Let go of the need to control. The moment you start worrying about *how* it will happen, you are moving out of trust and into resistance. Instead, shift your focus back to the present moment.

3. Follow the signs. When you trust, you become open to nudges, synchronicities, and guidance that will lead you in the right direction. The universe is always communicating with you - pay attention.

4. Detach from the outcome. Trust means holding the vision without clinging to it. It means being at peace whether it happens today, tomorrow, or in a year - because deep down, you know it's already done.

5. Lean into faith, not fear. Fear will tell you it's not working, that you need to *do more*, that you are running out of time. Trust reminds you that

you are exactly where you are meant to be, and everything is unfolding in divine perfection.

Manifestation is not just about taking action - it's about learning to let go and surrender with certainty. When you trust, you stay in alignment, keep your frequency high, and allow miracles to unfold.

Action Step: Strengthen Your Trust Muscle

For the next seven days, practice radical trust. Every time doubt creeps in, pause and ask yourself: *What would I do if I fully trusted that everything is unfolding in my favour?* **Would you relax? Would you enjoy the present moment more? Would you release the worry? Then - do exactly that.**

Each evening, write down at least one sign or synchronicity that showed up for you that day. The more you look for evidence that things are working out, the more you will see it.

Because when you trust, you stay in flow. And when you stay in flow, the universe can deliver your desires with ease.

This brings us to the final step of our CREATE journey.

CHAPTER 12

EXPAND BEYOND LIMITS

I am love. I am light. I am powerful.
I am a creator. I am here to create
my experience.

What if everything you've imagined for yourself so far is only a fraction of what's truly possible?

Your mind has been conditioned to think within limits - what's realistic, what's safe, what seems achievable from where you stand right now. But the truth is, you are far more powerful than you realise. The only thing keeping you from creating a limitless reality is your belief that there are limits in the first place.

You have already done so much with the level of energy and awareness you've had up until now - so **imagine what becomes possible when you expand into your full potential**.

This is where you stretch beyond your old identity, beyond the edges of what feels comfortable, beyond what you thought was available to you. This is where you step into the unknown, not with fear, but with excitement.

Because when you think bigger, you create bigger.

What Expanding Beyond Limits Looks Like

1. Stretch your vision beyond what feels comfortable. If what you desire still feels "possible," stretch it further. What would happen if you doubled it? Tripled it? Went beyond even that? Expansion starts when you move beyond what feels safe.

2. Train yourself to hold more. Many people can manifest success, but they struggle to sustain it because their energy contracts when they receive more than they're used to. Your job is to expand your capacity - to not only attract more abundance, love, and opportunity but to hold it with ease.

3. Reframe fear as growth. Your mind will try to pull you back into familiar territory - it will tell you expansion is risky, that you're not ready. This is not a sign to stop. It is a sign to keep going. Fear only arises when you are stepping into something greater.

4. Decide that your next level is inevitable. Expansion is not about *if* it will happen - it is about choosing that it already has. Act, think, and move through the world as if your biggest vision is already unfolding. When you hold that level of certainty, reality has no choice but to catch up.

5. Never settle. There is no final destination - only new levels of growth, joy, and possibility. Ev-

ery time you think you've hit your limit, stretch again. What's next? What else is possible? Expansion is infinite.

Action Step: Stretch Your Capacity

For the next seven days, challenge yourself to think and live bigger. Each morning, ask: *Where am I still thinking too small? How can I expand beyond this? What would happen if I went even further?* **Then, take one action each day that feels bigger than what your old self would have done.**

At the end of the week, reflect: Where did I stretch? How did it feel? What expanded as a result?

Because your life expands in direct proportion to the limits you are willing to break.

So here we are. You made it this far.

If you've read these pages, if you've felt these truths, if something deep within you is stirring, know this: it is not by accident. You have been called here for a reason.

Your soul has always known this path was yours to walk. The fact that you are here, that you have made it to this point, is proof that you are ready. Ready to awaken. Ready to step forward. Ready to create a life that reflects the truth of who you are.

This is your moment. Your only time is now. You are not here to live in limitation. You are not here to play small. You are here to be the living embodiment of your highest self. You are here to co-create with the infinite, to manifest your deepest desires, to align, embody, act, trust, and expand into the vastness of what is possible for you.

And now - you have the tools to do it.

This book was never just about learning. It was about **remembering**.

A remembering of who you are. A remembering of what is possible. A remembering of your infinite creative power.

But now, the real journey begins. Because it is not enough to simply understand these truths. You must **live them.**

YOUR NEXT STEPS

Everything you desire is already waiting for you. But it is **you** who must meet it halfway. It is **you** who must claim it. It is **you** who must take action.

Here's where you begin:

1. **Commit to the work.** Reading this book is just the first step. The real transformation happens when you apply what you've learned. Choose one practice - whether it's scribing, heart coherence, meditation, or aligned action - and commit to it daily.

2. **Remember who you are.** Any time doubt creeps in, any time fear tries to pull you back into smallness, come back to the truth. You are love. You are light. You are powerful. You are a creator. You are here to create your experience.

3. **Take the leap.** You don't need to know every step. You don't need to have it all figured out. You just need to begin. Move. Trust. Follow what lights you up, and the path will reveal itself.

4. **Expand beyond limits.** Do not settle for less than what you are capable of creating. Stretch your vision. Hold yourself to the highest expectation. Decide that your next level is inevitable.

5. **Let go of the outcome.** Your job is not to force things into place. Your job is to align with the energy, take inspired action, and then allow the universe to do its part. Trust that everything is unfolding exactly as it should.

A FINAL THOUGHT

If there's one thing I want you to take away from this book, it's this:

The universe is always listening. Your energy is always creating. You are always manifesting.

So the question is not whether you are manifesting. The question is:

Are you manifesting the life you want - or the life you are unconsciously settling for?

Every thought, every belief, every emotion, every action - it is all shaping your reality. The version of you who is living your dream life is not waiting for things to change. **They are choosing to love themselves now.** They are choosing to raise their vibration now. They are choosing to make the changes, day after day to improve their lives. Little by little, step by step, they are creating enormous change by choosing how to feel in this moment.

And now - it is your turn.

You are not here to play small. You are not here to struggle, to shrink, to settle. You are here to be a radiant, expansive force of creation. You are here to shine, to lead, to live in full expression of who you truly are.

The only thing left to do is decide.

Will you step through the door?

Will you claim the power that has always been yours?

Will you become the version of yourself who **knows** they are limitless?

It is time.

I can't wait to hear about how you have created the extraordinary!

This is only the beginning. If you are ready to take your transformation to the next level, I invite you to explore Life Activation, other healing or deeper spiritual coaching with me. I also run a membership community full of amazing women who are working on these shifts every day - we would love to welcome you!

You can find out more at **www.annaa.com** or reach out at **anna@annaa.com** and we can arrange a time to talk about creating a bespoke plan that works specifically for you.

Because this work is not meant to be done alone.

We rise together.

Printed in Dunstable, United Kingdom

67014797R00087